Hypnosis and The Law

Composite artist: Harlan Embrey, A.A., B.F.A., Scientific Investigation Division, Reno Police Department, Reno, Nevada.

A training-manual for the forensic and investigative uses of "trance" in law enforcement and legal practice

Published by WESTWOOD PUBLISHING COMPANY
312 RIVERDALE DRIVE, GLENDALE, CALIFORNIA 91204
(213) 242-3497

By Dr. Bradley William Kuhns

ISBN 0-930298-11-X

— FOREWORD —

Since hypnosis is now gaining nationwide acceptance as an important tool, not only in crime solving, but also in both criminal and civil litigation, this book is addressed to law enforcement officers, lawyers, and professional investigators.

In it are cited actual cases, showing how hypnosis is making notable contributions, and how you and others interested professionally in Human Behavior can utilize it most effectively.

For example, frequently in investigating a crime or a prospective legal case, an agent, a police officer or attorney will find himself frustrated by the victim, witness or client saying:

"I'm sorry, but I just can't remember."

When a victim of a crime or a lawyer's client offers that explanation it may be partial or almost total amnesia resulting from the traumatic shock of the crime or accident.

Often hypnosis provides a remedy — the only solution of the memory problem.

For all of us carry a recording of past experiences indelibly etched in our subconscious minds, and hypnosis can be used to delve into the subconscious and retrieve those blacked-out memories.

In many cases, even a reluctant witness can be induced to remember what he or she preferred to forget. The victim, who earnestly wishes to recall what happened, will usually not only recall while hypnotized many details previously forgotten when conscious, but will find the memory of the entire incident clearer. Consequently, he or she will be a much better witness in court.

By putting a witness in a trance and dredging deep into the witness' subconscious mind, police frequently get the important clues necessary to solve a crime. It may be an automobile license plate number that the witness could not otherwise recall, or an accurate description of the criminal offender — color, size, facial characteristics, voice, etc.

Likewise, investigators for a law firm or insurance company can use hypnosis to obtain information regarding an automobile accident that a client has difficulty remembering because of the traumatic nature of it. By hypnotizing the client and regressing him to the time of the accident, they may obtain an accurate statement of the situation — the position of the vehicles, traffic, and other factors.

In police work, the description of a criminal suspect, obtained from a witness under hypnosis, can be used to enable a staff artist to prepare a sketch. Such drawings published by the press have proved very effective.

Hypnotism is simply a natural mental process and is always safe, when done by trained persons. Contrary to some popular beliefs, a person in a hypnotic trance is not asleep or unconscious, nor likely to permit himself to be manipulated against his will. He is actually in a heightened state of awareness in which the mind's natural filter is temporarily bypassed, so that supressed memories are brought to the surface. And it is safe! No death certificate has ever recorded: "Died of hypnotism."

New York, Los Angeles, and many other police departments in both large and small cities are now using hypnosis to help solve crimes — *because it works.*

Having been both a student of hypnosis and investigative reporter covering crime and court cases for *The Los Angeles Times* and other newspapers, I enthusiastically endorse

iv

Dr. Kuhns' book, *Hypnosis and the Law.* The cases he cites are thoroughly documented, and his book is badly needed as a supplemental text for investigators. Especially those who have taken short training courses in hypnosis as an aid to crime solving will find it extraordinarily helpful.

William L. Roper

ABOUT DR. BRADLEY KUHNS

Dr. Kuhns has more than 20 years of professional level experience in the field of human behavior. He has served as consultant to Municipal, County, State and Federal agencies and in addition has acted as consultant to the medical and legal professions, and to institutions such as the American Institute of Hypnosis and the American College of Medical Hypnotists.

He is an author and lecturer, and earlier pursuits including studies in biological medicine, psychotherapy, teaching, military service and criminal investigation provide a rich and varied background for bringing technical-professional skill, practical understanding and rapport to his specialized field.

He is a member of: American Polygraph Association, American Association of Police Polygraphers, California Association of Polygraph Examiners, Society of Forensic and Investigative Hypnosis, and the Nevada Polygraph Association.

He is also listed in the 1980 "Who's Who in Law-Enforcement."

INTRODUCTION

by Gil Boyne, Executive Director,
American Council of Hypnotist Examiners

This book has been written because it is needed to supplement the meager training that is now being given law enforcement officers and special investigators in the use of hypnosis as a very important investigative tool.

At the present time the one recommended law enforcement training institute in this field on the West Coast only gives approximately thirty hours in its basic course and only twenty-two hours in its advanced course. This training is not enough to train an officer to be exceptionally proficient in the use of hypnotic techniques. And unfortunately, quite a part of the training course is given over to sessions of self-hypnosis, and other topics that really have no relevance to the actual needs of officers and special investigators. Something specific and more to the point is needed. They need more basic instruction in the everyday practical uses of hypnosis, especially in criminal investigations where crimes go unsolved because a witness cannot clearly remember. Hypnosis helps them remember. This book cites actual cases which hypnosis played a key role in solving. It shows how it is done.

So it is the purpose of this book to cut through all of the non-essential training materials and to offer the officer-investigator specific, helpful instruction technique in condensed form, deleting such things as history, self-hypnosis, etc. Such topics can be easily found in the many volumes on hypnosis that are available. It tells how to induce hypnosis and how to use it most effectively. Most importantly, it is written in an easy-to-read, non-technical language.

HYPNOSIS AND THE LAW

A workbook-manual for the
use of "trance" in law-enforcement
and legal practice

CHAPTER 1

CHAPTER 2

CHAPTER 3

CHAPTER 4

CHAPTER 5

CHAPTER I

HYPNOSIS – A TOOL FOR JUSTICE

Cases In Which Hypnosis Provided The Essential Clue

Hypnosis played a key role in helping solve one of the most shocking crimes in California history – the Chowchilla school bus kidnap case.

That nightmare began on the afternoon of July 15, 1976, when three masked, armed men hijacked the school bus, its driver and 26 summer school pupils just outside of Chowchilla, California, transferred the driver and children to two vans with covered windows, and took them about 100 miles to a rock quarry in Livermore, where they were buried alive in an underground prison – a large truck body planted in an excavation.

After spending one terrifying night in their windowless, underground prison, Frank Edward Ray, the 55-year-old bus driver, with the aid of the stronger pupils, managed to pry loose a heavy cover over a hole in the roof. He and his student-helpers then lifted out all of the children. A quarry worker led them to a telephone, so they could call for help. And they were all safely rescued.

For several days the crime, headlined in newspapers throughout America, remained a mystery. Who were the three masked men? Why had they done it?

As so often happens in such shocking criminal cases, victims and witnesses suffer a form of amnesia because of a traumatic experience, and are unable to remember details, or recall clearly things that aid law enforcement officials in identifying those committing the offense. This is a natural reaction of the human brain in many cases, because we all have a tendency to forget painful and unpleasant experiences.

Several of the students did recall pertinent facts. Yet after trying to interrogate many of the 26 children who had been kidnapped, finding them still shaken and confused, the investigating officers decided to concentrate on what clues they could obtain from Ray, the bus driver. Suffering from exhaustion and the trauma of the experience, Ray also had trouble remembering when first questioned.

This prompted Ed Bates, Madera County sheriff and a special agent for the FBI, to try using hypnosis as an aid to memory recall. So after conferring with fellow officials, he phoned Dr. William S. Kroger, a 72-year-old Beverly Hills psychiatrist and hypnotist, soliciting his assistance.

Convinced that hypnotism would help refresh his memory, Ray willingly cooperated. Dr. Kroger hypnotized Ray without difficulty, and with adroit questioning, led him mentally back over the events of the afternoon of July 15 when the kidnapping occurred.

At one point, Ray told of seeing a white van blocking the road and a masked man suddenly menacing him with a gun. Continuing to respond to Kroger's probing questions, Ray now remembered — what he had been unable to previously recall — the series of letters and numbers on the license plate of the white van blocking the roadway.

This license plate number proved to be the essential clue needed in tracking down the three kidnappers, and uncovering corroborating evidence. Arrested and convicted of kidnapping were: Richard Allen Schoenfeld, 22, his brother, James Leonard Schoenfeld, 24, and Fred Newhall Woods, 24. Woods, the last of the trio captured, was arrested in Vancouver, B.C. by Royal Mounted Officers. (To sharpen your own interrogation of victims and witnesses, under hypnosis, be sure to read "Question Guide" in Supplemental Data in back of book. It tells you questions to ask to get pertinent information needed.)

Hypnosis Effective In Solving Murder And Rape Cases

In recent years an increasing number of murder and rape crimes in California have been solved through leads obtained by hypnosis. Frequently information provided by victims and witnesses, under hypnosis, has enabled police artists to make accurate drawings of suspects that have led to arrests. (See Supplemental Data at back of book. It tells questions you should ask to get the best drawing.)

The Los Angeles Police Department's program using hypnosis to obtain investigative leads and significant evidence has resulted in solving 50 per cent of the cases assigned to it, according to officials. And police drawings made from details obtained from witnesses under hypnosis were found to be much superior to those made without hypnosis, they report. In one case, a composite drawing made from information obtained from a witness under hypnosis was found to be "almost photographic" in detail.

While simple memory recall can usually be achieved by a post hypnotic suggestion such as, "Now tell me about what happened on that particular night?" a deep hypnotic state is sometimes required to get the information desired. Then what is known as "revivification" regression is used. In revivification regression, the hypnotized person is led through a reenactment of a crucial crime or accident scene as if it were actually taking place.

It sometimes requires a well-developed level of hypnosis, and is used in cases where the victim or witness cannot remember significant information without hypnosis. IT IS DIRECTED EXCLUSIVELY TO GETTING EVIDENCE FROM VICTIMS OR WITNESSES IN IMPORTANT CASES, except in a most unusual case where a judge permits a defendant to be hypnotized in court. *Law enforcement officers should never hypnotize suspects, as it may be viewed as violating the suspect's civil rights.*

In one recent Los Angeles case, a young woman, who had been kidnapped and raped by three men, was so emotionally disturbed by the traumatic experience, she could provide little information until hypnotized. Under hypnosis, she recalled the names her rapists had called each other and various places they mentioned when conversing with each other. Also she remembered that one of them had mentioned being on a methadone program, and that one of them who had been in prison spoke of having friends in northern California. She also gave the police artist detailed descriptions of the three. When the three were later captured, the police drawings were found to be surprisingly accurate.

In fact, the police drawings made by L.A.P.D. artists from hypnotized witnesses during the long investigations of "Hillside Stranglings" were discovered to resemble Kenneth Bianchi, subsequently arrested in Bellingham, Washington. According to *The Los Angeles Times* of June 4, 1979, he has talked about murders under hypnosis, or apparent hypnosis, but credits them to his "split personality," which he identifies as "Steve Walker."

Bianchi has been charged with five of the strangler murders in southern California in addition to the two for which he faces charges in Washington. He is expected to plead insanity.

His case appears to provide another demonstration of how hypnosis may be used in formulating defense in a first degree murder case, in his — a dual personality.

Whatever the outcome of the Bianchi case, the fact that Los Angeles' large force of law officers assigned to the strangler investigation failed to successfully pursue the clues provided by hypnotized witnesses may continue to haunt the L.A.P.D. for some time. It had a good likeness of him sketched by a police artist.

When the body of one of the strangler's victims, Kimberly Ann Martin, 17, of West Hollywood, was found on December 15, 1978 in the Echo Park area, police investigation revealed she had been lured by a phone call to an apartment complex in Hollywood. The day before the Martin girl's murder, a man had called at the apartment house posing as a potential tenant. The apartment house manager showed him apartment 114. It was to that apartment that Miss Martin was lured by a phone call. From persons who said they had seen the suspect, the police got details of his appearance, under hypnosis.

This case points up the need to follow through on police leads obtained by hypnosis. Hypnosis alone cannot solve crimes. You must ask your subject the right question. (See Supplemental Data.) It requires diligent investigative checking to corroborate.

One such case involved the witnesses to a robbery at a Montgomery Ward store in Eagle Rock, California. Two men with guns forced the counting room employees to lie down on the floor, while they scooped up fifty-two thousand dollars in cash and script. They were observed by a number of witnesses, some who saw them eating breakfast in the store cafeteria and others who saw them as they left the store. After several hours of questioning by the police, the chief of security for Ward's, Mr. Thomas Rhodes, suggested that Mr. Gil Boyne, a noted Hypnotherapist, be called in to interrogate the witnesses under hypnosis.

Several significant changes in testimony were elicited while the witnesses were in hypnosis. The employee who opened the counting room door when the robbers knocked had told the police the man who first approached him with a gun was clean shaven. When hypnotized, he recalled that the man had a several-days' growth of beard in the area of the chin, as though he were trying to grow a goatee. The witnesses who saw the men leaving the store said they had a black fibreboard case, and the employee who opened the door for them agreed. Under hypnosis they remembered a blue airline flight bag with two words stenciled in white on the back which was carried by the second man. Several other significant changes in testimony were elicited under hypnosis. One man remembered a license number on an automobile he had seen parked on the store parking lot as the store was opening two weeks previous to the robbery. This turned out to be a stolen plate, but his detailed description of the car and its occupants while he was under hypnosis led to the apprehension of two men, one of whom had sixteen thousand dollars on his person, which was confiscated. One of the men was on parole after serving a sentence for armed robbery.

Hypnosis Helps Solve Fresno Rape Case

On June 28, 1977, Miss Norma Milligan, 15, and her 7-year-old cousin, Christina Alcorn, were strolling through a Fresno shopping mall when a strange man approached them.

"Your mother has been injured in an automobile accident," he told the younger girl, "and I've volunteered to take you to the hospital to see her."

Miss Milligan hesitated, reluctant to get in the stranger's car. But when the younger girl began to cry, she agreed to do so.

Soon after getting on the freeway, the man told them that he was a member of the Symbionese Liberation Army and that he was kidnapping them.

"If you try to escape," he threatened, "I'll burn your parents' homes."

During the four days the girls were held hostage, he raped the older girl. Then he drove them to Bakersfield where he released them at the Greyhound bus station. Miss Milligan phoned her home and police aid was sought.

When the police were unable to obtain any satisfactory clues to the identity of the kidnapper-rapist by questioning the girls, an investigator suggested hypnotizing Miss Milligan. Under hypnosis, she recalled that their abductor had stopped at a service station to have his car's air-conditioner repaired. FBI agents, working with police, found the service station where the work was done and traced ownership to Louis Adolfo Barbosa, pastor of the Zion Apostolic Temple in Hayward. He was identified by the girls as their abductor.

On December 13, 1977, Barbosa, 31, was found guilty of three counts of rape and two counts of sexual perversion against Miss Milligan when tried before Superior Judge Hollis Best. The defense presented no evidence or closing argument.

Another case, a murder, which a few years ago would have probably gone unsolved, was unraveled by Los Angeles police in 1977 by using hypnosis. Four girls out hitchhiking had been picked up by two men and driven to an apartment house after a long, rambling, circuitous route through a strange part of town that completely disoriented them. They suddenly realized they were in trouble when the man made aggressive sexual advances and one girl, who resisted, was shot and killed. The other three managed to escape and report the killing.

But because of the trauma of the experience and the fact that they had been in an unfamiliar part of the city, they were unable to identify the apartment or its location. The investigating officers decided to try hypnosis.

"While under hypnosis, one of the girls remembered quite a few details — a description of the exterior of the apartment house and surrounding buildings," Captain Michael Nielson explained later. Aided by this information, police found the apartment. Just as they were taking the girls in, a resident of the apartment came down the hall. The girls immediately identified him as one of the two men sought.

Nielson, director of the L.A.P.D.'s investigative program and president of the Society for Investigative and Forensic Hypnosis, is an enthusiastic supporter of the use of hypnosis in solving criminal cases. By relaxing a victim or a witness, it enables them to concentrate on details that would escape them during a routine interview, he explains.

"When one consciously tenses up, the information becomes elusive," he said.

Numerous Cities Now Using Hypnosis To Combat Crime

New York citizens have been marveling at the success its police department has achieved recently in cracking puzzling criminal cases, since the police department employed Sgt.

Charles Diggett as its official hypnotist. Diggett, 51, has helped solve approximately 120 cases since employed in 1976. His exploits have resulted in national publicity for the department.

In the East Bay community of Concord, Calif., Detective Chief Larry Haines is winning similar recognition for using hypnosis successfully in unlocking the memories of witnesses to get significant crime clues. Although he only learned much of his hypnotic skill at a training course in May, 1977, he has been called into investigations to solve mystifying cases in Vallejo, Berkeley, Walnut Creek, Brentwood, Pleasant Hill and the Contra Costa county sheriff's office.

He predicts that within a decade virtually all Bay Area police agencies will be using hypnosis. Approximately 90 per cent more information can be obtained by questioning under hypnosis than in old traditional methods, he declares.

Haines also has a good word for the therapeutic value of hypnosis, that it has lowered his blood pressure and that he finds it can be used to relieve victims' "traumas connected with crime," especially rape victims.

From Amarillo, Texas, Kansas City, Mo., Hutchinson, Kansas, and other cities, have come recent reports of puzzling murder and rape cases being solved by the use of hypnosis investigative techniques.

FBI Now Using Hypnosis

In certain major cases, in which victims and witnesses give their consent, they are now being hypnotized by specially trained FBI agents, acting under strict guidelines.

"The bureau wants the public to know exactly what we are doing," explained Chicago FBI Agent Robert Scigalski in Chicago, when questioned about the agency's new training program for "hypnosis technicians."

"In June, 1978, Scigalski and 58 other agents from FBI field offices attended the FBI Training Academy in Quantico, Va. for a four-day seminar on the theory, history and uses of hypnosis in interviewing witnesses."

Hypnosis More Than Investigative Clue-Finding Tool

Despite the wide use now being made by police of hypnosis as an important investigative tool to find clues that a victim or witness has trouble recalling, it has other primary functions in criminal cases.

For instance, it can be used as:

(1) An analytical process to assist in finding an individual's attitude or state of mind prior to, or at the time of a crime (or in other words was malice a part of the mental state?)

(2) Or as a defense in a criminal case. (The Bianchi case, mentioned earlier, in which a split-personality has been indicated under hypnosis.)

(3) Or as a means of developing leads for additional evidence from witnesses.

For years California courts refused to admit evidence obtained under hypnosis. But now that is changed. Records show that the first case leading to admission of evidence obtained through hypnosis was that of Cornell vs. Superior Court of San Diego (52 Cal. 2nd 99, May 1959). Attorney Richard Cornell petitioned the California Supreme Court to compel the San Diego court and sheriff's office to permit his client, Paul LeClair Conrey, to employ a hypnotist for needed medical aid in preparing a defense for Conrey, who was charged with murder. Such assistance, Cornell argued, was necessary because his client's memory was impaired by alcohol and age. He could not remember whether or not he had caused the death of a young woman with whom he had been drinking. The court granted Cornell's petition. But when hypnotized, Conrey's memory was still unclear. He was found guilty of manslaughter, but was later exonerated when another confessed responsibility for the woman's death.

One case often mentioned as demonstrating how hypnosis has been successfully used in defense of a person charged with murder is the trial of Arthur C. Nebb of Ohio. He was hypnotized in court in Columbus, Ohio, in June 1962 (the first time this was ever done), and allowed to tell under hypnosis how he shot his estranged wife and Estel J. Stepp. Stepp died, Mrs. Nebb lived. Another case illustrating use of hypnosis in court was that of Mrs. Gladys Lillian Pitt of British Columbia, who was hypnotized in the presence of a jury when tried on a charge of attempting to murder her husband with a hammer. Following her testimony, the charge of attempted murder was changed to assault, and she was given only a one-year sentence. In Nebb's case, the charge of first degree murder was reduced to manslaughter. He was sentenced to from one to 20 years in the Ohio penitentiary — a sentence that made him eligible for parole in eight months.

However, during the Nebb trial, Dr. T. R. Huxtable, who hypnotized Nebb, admitted that he had hypnotized Nebb twice previously, and testifying as an expert witness, said that testimony obtained under hypnosis was usually reliable. He later qualified this latter statement, explaining this would not be true in cases involving persons with certain types of mental disorders. Several outstanding authorities on hypnosis now question that opinion of Dr. Huxtable that statements made under hypnosis are usually true. While they hold that hypnosis is an excellent means of getting information during an investigation, they believe that a guilty person could lie about his guilt while hypnotized.

The fact that Huxtable had hypnotized Nebb twice prior to Nebb's testimony in court also raises another legal objection to its acceptance as true. During the prior hypnosis, the defendant could have been instructed regarding what to say. Consequently, hypnotizing a defendant in court remains a tricky strategy, subject to close legal scrutiny.

Fifteen years after his conviction of manslaughter in Ohio in 1962, Nebb, in recent years a resident of Huntington Park, California, has been convicted and sentenced to prison for soliciting his brother to kill the son of his former wife and maim a woman who was a close friend of his ex-wife. In 1977 he was given a two-to-10 year prison sentence. His recent trial was before Superior Judge Bonnie Lee Martin in Los Angeles.

A court order to allow a person accused of murder to be hypnotized grew out of the Cornell vs. San Diego court case. It is known as No. A-104699.

Five uses of hypnosis in adjudicating legal cases are obvious. They are:

(1) To get, if possible, a truthful account of an incident or a series of related events from a witness.

(2) To enable a witness to recall incidents no longer in his conscious memory.

(3) To detect malingerers, who are pretending to have an illness or injury.

(4) To weed out witnesses who have given false and misleading information about a crime or accident before being hypnotized.

(5) To discover if hypnosis or some form of secret influence was used to commit a crime or to evade conviction.

Use of Hypnosis in Civil Cases

The above cited uses of hypnosis are applicable in civil as well as criminal cases. In fact, hypnosis is currently being used in investigating medical malpractice suits and insurance claims arising from automobile, airplane, and industrial accidents.

For instance, hypnosis has been successfully employed in finding the cause of airplane crashes. One pilot, under hypnosis, told how he had caused a crash that had occurred many years previously, an accident that had mystified investigators at the time. At the time "fatigue and lack of alertness on the part of the pilot" had been suspected. But under hypnosis, the pilot revealed that he had been unfamiliar with the new type altimeter and mistrusting it, had made an airport landing much too low, striking nearby trees.

HOW TO HYPNOTIZE

Use Pre-Induction Talk to Gain Subject's Confidence

Although everyone can be hypnotized to some degree, some much easier than others, occasionally you will find a person who may be difficult because he or she is afraid, lacks confidence in you or has difficulty concentrating. So a pre-induction talk is often necessary to alleviate any fears the subject may have and win his or her confidence.

Keep in mind: as a law enforcement officer *you will never be called upon to hypnotize suspects* — only victims and witnesses.

Because some persons, both illiterate and the well-educated still retain some negative conceptions of hypnosis as being related to sinister black magic and others relate it to vaudeville hocus pocus, it is often necessary to explain that such images of it are completely wrong. Hypnotism gained part of its association with black magic from *Trilby,* a novel written by George Du Maurier in 1894, in which a villainous hypnotist, Svengali, played a prominent role in casting a spell over Trilby, an art model.

Of course, this negative image of hypnosis is unfortunate, for today it is being used for society's safety by aiding in the solution of criminal cases. It is also being used as an auxiliary to medicine in the treatment of disease and as anesthesia. It is neither sinister nor dangerous. In fact, never has any potential for danger been documented.

This is a point that the hypno-investigator needs to get across to the mind of his subject before starting to induce hypnosis. For first of all the person to be hypnotized needs to have confidence in hypnosis, and confidence in you, the operator.

Hypnosis Is Easy, If —

Hypnosis is simply a technique for developing a relaxed mental state in another person by suggestion.

To become a successful hypno-investigator, you must have confidence in yourself and your ability. You must never tell anyone you want to hypnotize that you are a beginner. If you have had the training, rely on that training. And, *you must most always speak in an authoritative tone of voice and use positive words and phrases.* In fact, you yourself must believe you cannot fail, and avoid any negative suggestion of failure. If you are practicing induction in the presence of others, *ignore the doubters and hecklers.* Even if you have failed in your first efforts to hypnotize, you are NOT a failure. You can *blame the failure on your subject's inability to cooperate, if cooperation was indeed lacking.*

So begin your induction in a friendly, confident, professional manner. For best results, select a quiet room, where you will not be distracted by street or office noises. Bright lights can also be distracting. *Remember — speak clearly, distinctly and confidently — and with a serious, sincere manner.*

Learn many induction processes and use the one that seems to fit the subject. Practice will enable you to develop an inductive routine that will work best for you.

Obtaining Voluntary Cooperation

Since your witness has agreed to be hypnotized to achieve better memory recall as an aid to investigation, you can use what is known as "the permissive approach" explaining that he or she will be in complete control and that "you will not have to proceed unless you want to." When "the authoritarian approach" is used, the subject can be made to feel that he will respond automatically.

13

Continuing with Pre-Conditioning

Here is what you can say to put your subject in a receptive frame of mind: (Variations — in Supplemental Data at back of book.)

"Please don't rationalize or analyze as I am giving you instructions. Just listen closely, follow along and allow things to happen. You'll never be unconscious. You'll hear everything I say at all times. Should anything of an emergency nature occur, *you can arouse yourself immediately.* I want you to follow along with me. You may hear sounds inside or outside the room, but those sounds are not going to bother you. You may even hear a phone ring. You may hear a car pass or some other street noise. But none of these every day outside noises are going to affect your concentration.

"For you will focus on my voice and what I am saying to you. These other sounds, when you hear them will only help you relax more and help you go deeper to sleep. It is going to be a pleasant, relaxing experience. You are doing fine. I require cooperation on your part. Other than that I ask nothing of you. In fact, you are going to feel very relaxed and free of everyday tensions. Hypnosis is refreshing. It is simply a state of healthful relaxation induced by my suggestions. When you are into hypnosis, you will be able to remember things more clearly than usual because your mind will be able to concentrate much more easily."

Pre-Induction Talk for a Group

"Your ability to be hypnotized will depend entirely upon your willingness to cooperate. It has nothing to do with your intelligence. As for your willpower, you can remain fully aware all of the time and not pay attention to anything I'm saying. If, on the other hand, you pay close attention to what I say and follow what I tell you, you can relax and enter the hypnotic state. By doing so, you will be helping yourself to a warm, wonderful form of relaxation you may not have thought possible.

"Hypnosis is neither unnatural nor supernatural. It is merely a relaxed condition that enables one to concentrate on some particular thing. In a sense, you are hypnotized whenever you focus intently on a good movie, and forget you are a part of the audience and feel you are part of the story.

"Your cooperation and interest is all I ask. As I have said, the ability to be hypnotized rests with you. You will hear everything and be aware of everything that goes on around you. Just remain as passive as possible, listen to what I say, do not try to analyze or help me in any way. Nor should you try to resist. Just let things happen. Nothing will be said or done to embarrass you in any way."

Having once hypnotized a person or group, you will find it easier to hypnotize them a second or third time, since they will have increased confidence and responsiveness to your suggestions.

How to Induce Hypnosis: Induction Technique

There are numerous proven methods of hypnotic induction. Most of them work equally well, although most experienced hypnotists have a favored procedure of their own. In principle they are all very similar, relying upon the use of certain words and phrases that have suggestibility for inducing the state of hypnosis desired.

Here is one of the standard procedures:

Select a quiet room if possible where you will have little disturbance.

Ask your subject to make himself comfortable in a chair or on a sofa, and have him place his hands loosely on his lap or alongside his body. When he is comfortably located, you speak to him clearly and in a commanding tone as follows:

"Now I want you to take a deep breath and let it out slowly, relaxing your body more than before. Close your eyes and listen closely to my words and instructions. I want you to concentrate upon what I am saying and to shut out most other thoughts.

"Now concentrate on an imaginary spot in the center of your forehead. Where I touch you gently on the forehead, an imaginary spot will form. As you concentrate on that imaginary spot, serene calm, comfort and relaxation will begin to occur throughout your body. And this relaxation occurs in almost everyone. That calm, serene feeling of relaxation will begin with the muscles in the top of your scalp. That relaxation will gently move down over your forehead; down over all your facial muscles; your eyes and cheeks; down over all your neck muscles; going deeper relaxed, becoming more calm and serene, as the feeling moves down over your chest; on through to your waist; feeling still more relaxed than ever, over your hips and into your thighs . . . . In fact, you can feel you total body becoming very, very relaxed. It may even feel cool and light, calm and comfortable. As you listen to my voice, you may begin to notice the weight of your body. Your legs will become very heavy, very tired and pleasantly warm . . . your arms will become very heavy, very tired and pleasantly warm . . . your neck, shoulders and head will also become very heavy, very tired and pleasantly warm. Your eyes may be closing even tighter. And, you're becoming more dreamy and drowsy and more sleepy. As you continue to relax, nothing more than the relaxing, steady sounds of my voice carry you deeper toward a very restful, relaxing, comfortable, dreamy, drowsy, sleep. As you bring your attention back to that spot on your forehead, your mind is wandering and dreaming as if you were gradually becoming lighter and lighter. As you are relaxed all over, parts of your body may even be growing heavier than others. Even more tired than other parts. And, as those changes are happening, you are drifting still deeper and down, down, deeper and deeper into sleep, a calm, dreamless sleep. In a moment, you will be in the most comfortable, calm, welcome, relaxed state you have ever known.

"You are now completely relaxed all over . . . . You are going even deeper into sleep, until I give you the signal to awaken. It is a peaceful, restful sleep.

"You are going even deeper to sleep . . . deeper, deeper, and deeper. Now you are in a deep hypnotic state."

The above words are usually sufficient to hypnotize the average subject, but in some cases, it may be necessary to repeat some of the phrases. (See Induction Variations in Supplemental Data at back of book.)

Other Methods of Induction

Dr. James Braid, the English physician, who first discovered that persons could be hypnotized by suggestion while having them gaze steadily and intently at a bright shining object, recommended that form of induction. Spinning discs and many other devices have since been used to tire the eye muscles and accelerate the hypnotic process. But virtually the same effect can be achieved by having one's subject gaze fixedly at a spot on the wall or his own thumb.

In case you choose to use one of these technics, you simply command your subject to fix his eyes on some object and continue to stare at it, while you suggest that he is starting to relax and can close his eyes when they become tired.

Then you would add: "Now keep your eyes closed and continue to relax. Just let yourself go. Let all of the tension drain out of your body. Listen to my voice and pay no attention to anything else. Just relax and listen to what I am saying. Now focus your attention on your scalp and let the muscles of your scalp become completely relaxed, etc."

You can follow through with suggestions, as in the first procedure cited. (You can also interchange with suggested methods in Supplemental Data at the back of the book.)

There are different states of hypnosis: (1) Light, (2) Medium, and (3) Deep. Usually in a light state of hypnosis, a subject will not be able to open his eyes, if told in a commanding voice, he cannot. If he can open his eyes, it will be after an obvious effort.

In a medium state, he will not be able to open his eyes

17

upon being told he cannot do so. He can be given post-hypnotic suggestions in this state. He will be partially aware of what is going on around him, and his memory may be vague. Memory appears to depend upon the person, it may vary from full memory to complete blank.

You, the hypno-investigator, may test the degree or depth of the hypnosis by challenges, like: "Now you are so deeply and comfortably relaxed that your eyelids are stuck shut. You may try to open your eyes, and the more you try, the tighter they stay shut." (To determine the hypnotic depth check reflective signs as detailed in Supplemental Data in back of book.)

If your subject opens his eyes, further hypnotic induction is required. If he cannot open them or has difficulty, he is in a light state of hypnosis. In that case, you say: "You can stop trying to open your eyes, for you are now hypnotized and feeling just fine. I am going to begin counting to ten, and as I slowly count, you will be going deeper and deeper into hypnosis."

Then you count: *"One,* you are going deeper and deeper . . . *two,* deeper, deeper . . . *three,* you are getting more and more relaxed and going deeper, deeper asleep, (and so on, until) *ten* . . . you are now very deep, deeply hypnotized and feeling just wonderful in every way."

At this point, you can repeat your eye challenge test.

Deepening Hypnosis by Arm Lowering

"Now I'm going to take you even deeper into trance," you can tell the subject, and instead of just counting as explained above, you can start by taking hold of his wrist and raising his forearm and saying: "Now I am going to raise your forearm and count from ten to zero as I lower it. As I lower your arm and count, you will go more deeply into hypnosis. When your arm is completely lowered, you will be in a very deep relaxed trance."

Then as you proceed to lower his arm, you count slowly,

starting with ten and counting to zero, suggesting at every count that he is going deeper and deeper into hypnosis.

While your subject is in hypnosis, you should reinforce your hypnotic control by giving him a post-hypnotic suggestion, such as "now and hereafter, each and every time I suggest hypnosis to you, you easily and quickly reenter this state."

Or you can say: "In the future, whenever I count from one to five, you will go into this same kind of relaxing trance quickly and easily. Upon the count of five you will enter hypnotic sleep, just as you are now." (Another deepening technique in Supplemental Data at back of book.)

Different States of Recall

Since much of your use of hypnosis will probably be during investigations to enable a witness to recall significant information that he or she cannot remember when conscious, it should be pointed out that it is not always necessary to put the subject in the deepest state of hypnosis. Often the subject's memory of the incident under investigation will substantially improve while in a light or medium state of hypnosis. It is sometimes felt advisable to try obtaining the information in one of these lighter stages of hypnosis, when it does not seem to be necessary to lead the subject back into a mental re-enactment of the scene with its traumatic potentials for him.

But where the desired information is of prime importance in solving an important criminal case, such as identifying an auto license plate number or obtaining descriptions of a murder suspect, a deeper level of hypnosis is often required. Then a mental re-enactment of the scene of the crime, called a "revivification" or "scene visualization" will often enable the hypnotized witness to recall vividly the picture of the incident stored in his subconscious mind.

By using revivification, time expansion and scene visualization techniques, the hypnotist was able to obtain the license number of the kidnappers' getaway van in the Chowchilla school bus kidnapping mentioned earlier.

To do this the subject is regressed backward in time to the day and hour of the incident under investigation. Hypermnesia is the term used in referring to the recovery of information or in increase of memory recall beyond that possible through non-hypnotic methods. But there is a difference between hypermnesia and what is known as revivification, the hypnotic state in which the subject is caused to relive mentally an incident as if it were actually taking place. The revivification process for the subject is like watching a television show of the incident, and the operator can stop the show at a given point, tell the subject to concentrate on the license plate of a car or the facial characteristics of the chief suspect.

When Frank Ed Ray, the driver of the Chowchilla school bus, was under hypnosis and going through a revivification of the bus hijacking, Ray mentioned seeing the road ahead of him blocked by a white van. The hypnotist stopped the mental motion picture at that point and asked Ray to take a close look at the license plate of the van. Ray was able to read off all of the digits on the license plate except one. This license plate number was the clue that led to the kidnappers of the Chowchilla school children.

How to Regress Subject to Past Crime Scene

When the hypnotist, is satisfied that his subject is in a deep state of hypnosis, such as required for revivification, he may suggest that he wants the subject to picture himself at home watching television. You may use the following suggestion:

"Now the picture that will start showing on your TV in a minute or two will be a replay of that crime (or accident) you saw (give date and location, if known) and I want you to describe what you see as the action occurs. When I count three, the picture will begin showing on your TV screen."

Count three, "Now I'm turning on the TV and it's warming up, (count three) what do you see? Tell me when the picture starts."

If revivification is starting to work, the subject will begin describing the scene, stopping at the request of the hypnotist to focus upon some detail — a face, an article of clothing, a weapon or a license plate. (Consult Supplemental Data for more on this — especially what questions to ask of subject.)

In case the subject becomes too excited or involved in what he is seeing, the hypnotist places a gentle, sympathetic hand on his shoulder and assures him: "It's all right. It's just a re-run."

Such mental re-runs under hypnosis are often painful for victims of traumatic crimes, and care must be taken to soothe and calm the subject. If the experience becomes too painful or frightening for the subject, the show can be terminated and the subject dehypnotized after being assured he is going to feel "totally relaxed and refreshed." In a later hypnotic session, he may become less disturbed and recall the information needed.

Getting good results sometimes requires practice and experimentation. It is often comforting to tell subjects in the very beginning: "Hypnosis is really a form of self-hypnotism. I have no power over you."

Yet there are illiterate, ignorant persons — and possibly some highly intellectual, who like to think that you do have some mysterious, magical power, and are more suggestible to hypnosis as a result of this belief. So that is a point to consider in analyzing your best approach to a subject's cooperation. There are, of course, no persons who cannot be hypnotized to some degree, but a few may be difficult, either because they refuse to cooperate due to fears or misconceptions, or are lacking in imagination.

How to Terminate the Trance

The process for dehypnotizing a person should probably be learned first, so that you can reassure persons who have

21

some fear they may "not be brought out of it."

But actually, as many other hypnosis experts point out, this is a groundless fear. Spontaneous dehypnotization invariably occurs, even if the subject had been given a contrary suggestion. In fact, a hypnotized person will often awaken if the operator leaves the room. And a subject if given a suggestion that he finds objectionable may suddenly awake. (Make certain to give proper post-hypnotic suggestions. See information regarding this in Supplemental Data.)

There are several well-known techniques for smoothly and gently awakening a person from hypnosis. Perhaps, one of the best is to use a counting process as follows:

"You will gradually become fully aware as I begin counting slowly from one to five. When I reach the count of five, you are fully aware and feeling clear-headed and refreshed in body and mind. ONE, you are slowly and calmly returning to your full awareness. TWO, you are becoming more and more aware. THREE, your eyes are ready to open. FOUR, now you are fully aware and your eyes are fully open. FIVE, you are fully aware and feeling good in every way.

Not often, but occasionally, a hypnotized person is enjoying the peaceful relaxation so much, he or she may be reluctant to terminate trance. In case they are slow in waking up completely, say, "One, two, three — Ready!! FULLY AWARE!" in a loud, commanding voice, and clap your hands.

Of course, you could let a person, who may be needing a good sleep, just sleep it off, for the person will wake up in a few hours.

Remember success in hypnotizing depends mainly on self-confidence and positive suggestions given in a firm, confident and usually no-nonsense tone of voice. Suggestions must be clearly worded. (Be sure to read Supplemental Data, regarding induction and dehypnotizing.)

IMPORTANT RULES TO KEEP IN MIND

1. In giving suggestions always use simple, clearly stated words and phrases that can be easily understood.

2. State the suggestions in the form of a direct request.

3. Always use positive words . . . never negative.

4. Use the second person in addressing subject, such as: "You will do this or that . . . ."

5. Remember to cancel out all suggestions of a post-suggestive nature before awakening subject.

6. To induce a subject to see any mental picture or scene clearly, "You can now see . . . ."

7. The deeper the hypnosis, the more effective your suggestions.

8. Most hypnotized subjects will resist and reject suggestions that they think may threaten them in any way or create conflicts with their value systems or character attitudes. People have a wide variety of fears, which might cause them to resist certain suggestions. For example, if you suggested to a subject with claustrophobia that he was now going to get in an elevator or small room, he might recoil from the suggestion, and awake.

9. Keep your suggestions realistic. Don't say "When I snap my fingers you will be standing on the street and no longer on the fifteenth floor of that insurance building." Instead say: "You can see yourself walking toward the escalators and can vividly see the sign by the escalator which indicates you are on the fifteenth floor. Now you are going to take that escalator down to the street level." (This can be used in giving suggestions that subject is going deeper and deeper to sleep.)

10. Hypnosis is a mental state wherein the subject's atten-

tion is channeled and is usually narrowed and focused upon one area of concern, selectively ignoring all others.

IMPORTANT PRECAUTIONS – PLAY IT SAFE .

1. Hypnosis is a serious matter . . . be careful of suggestions given persons under hypnosis. Never give any that might prove harmful.

2. Never leave alone any person you have hypnotized. Stay with him until he is awake and is definitely dehypnotized. It is wise to remain with him a short time after he wakes up to be sure. A person in any degree of hypnotism is not consciously aware of the many potential dangers around him, for his attention is narrowed and focused totally upon the operator and the suggestions the operator has given him. For instance, if you permitted a person still under hypnosis to walk from a building into the street without assistance, a fatal or serious accident might result.

3. If a hypnotized person is on his feet, tell him to stand still and not wander around, unless it is necessary that he move a short distance under the operator's suggestions.

4. Before touching subject or making any physical contact with him during the process of induction, be sure to tell him in advance. Any unexpected move on your part might cause him to terminate his trance and re-hypnotization could be difficult. To prevent a problem of this kind, you might give him a suggestion, phrased something like this: "Pay no heed if I accidentally touch. Nothing that I do will bother or cause you any discomfort in any way."

5. Do not use your hypnotic skills as a police officer to "treat" fellow officers for medical or psychological ailments. Remember, you are a specialist in using hypnosis for investigative purposes.

CHAPTER II

ELEVEN RECOMMENDED STEPS FOR
THE HYPNO-INVESTIGATOR

The supplemental data includes the recommended 11 steps for the hypno-investigator to follow. For best results, it is suggested and recommended that the hypno-investigator follow the steps and procedures in the recommended order so that an in-depth hypnosis session is the final result. So, to summarize:

STEP NUMBER 1: Interview subject, take notes for any information pertaining to the issue at hand (using supp. form) (out of hypnosis).

STEP NUMBER 2: Have the subject sign the release form, giving their permission to undergo the hypnosis session.

STEP NUMBER 3: Pre-Induction Explanation to the subject (as needed).

STEP NUMBER 4: (RME) Responsive Mental Exercises

STEP NUMBER 5: Hypnotic Induction

STEP NUMBER 6: Challenges - Suggestions (as needed, checking depth).

STEP NUMBER 7: Deepening procedure (as needed) (somnambulistic stage if possible).

STEP NUMBER 8: (I.S.S.) Instant Sleep Suggestion to re-hypnotize.

STEP NUMBER 9: Operator (O.C.) takes control to issue suggestions for information retrieval, descriptions, artist sketch, post-hypnotic suggestions, etc. (use supp. form) (in hypnosis).

STEP NUMBER 10: (R/R) Return and Remove. First removing any unwanted suggestions. Then, following through with a wake-up procedure, bringing the subject out of hypnosis.

STEP NUMBER 11: Show concern. After bringing the subject out of the hypnotic state, stay with the subject and listen to the subject. Answer any questions that the subject may have.

HYPNOSIS RETRIEVAL INFORMATION SHEET
– PART ONE –

Case No.:_____ Crime:_____

Agency:_____

Date:_____ Subject:_____

DOB:_____ Sex:_____

Address: (residence)_____

Telephone: (residence)_____

Address: (business)_____

Telephone: (business)_____

Marital Status:_____

Occupation:_____ How Long:_____

Volunteer for hypnosis: (yes)   (no)

Ever hypnotized before:_____ times?

Have you ever had a serious (injury) (accident) (illness) ?

Explain:_____

Are you on any drugs or medications at the present time?

Explain:_____

Are you under a doctor's care at the present time? (yes) (no)

Explain:_____

Use HRI sheet parts one and two during the pre-hypnosis phase of the interview.

HYPNOSIS RETRIEVAL INFORMATION SHEET
– PART TWO –

Were there any prior hypnotic sessions required relating to the current case at issue? (yes) (no) If so, Explain:

_____

Is subject: Victim, Witness, (Other, Explain): _____

_____

Time Session Began: _____Time Terminated: _____

Hypno-Investigator: _____

Address of Session: _____

Is session being monitored? _____

How? _____ (Video/Tape/Other) _____

ID# _____

Persons present during hypnotic session: _____

_____

_____

_____

ADDITIONAL NOTE AND COMMENTS:

Use HRI sheet parts one and two during the pre-hypnosis phase of the interview.

CONSENT/RELEASE FORM   *STEP 2*

DATE:_____

TIME: _____

I _____ , do hereby voluntarily without objections, agree freely with full cooperation to undergo hypnosis, questioning and interrogation under hypnosis and understand the interviews and sessions may be mechanically sound recorded or video taped. Permission is hereby granted for the hypnosis session as described above in

order to assist the_____ Department/Agency with an investigation currently in progress.

I also understand that I may be required to subsequently participate in this type of interview and hypnotic session for further verification purposes, to which I agree now and during the length of the ongoing investigation.

I further release and discharge_____ , and the operator of all claims of every kind and nature, known and unknown by reason of said hypnosis sessions and interview and consent, agree and direct that the results of such interview and hypnosis session shall be made known to

_____

_____

SIGNATURE: _____

ADDRESS: _____

WITNESS: _____

HYPNOSIS RELEASE FORM
(SIMPLE)

STEP 2

I,_____, do hereby request
and agree to be placed under hypnosis by:　__HYPNOTIST,__
__INVESTIGATIVE__　and I offer my cooperation and make
this request without any threat of punishment, compulsion,
or promise of any type of reward whatsoever.

SUBJECT:_____

INVESTIGATIVE
HYPNOTIST:_____

WITNESS: _____

WITNESS:_____

DATE: _____

HYPNOSIS MINOR RELEASE FORM   *STEP 2*

I, _____ , hereby certify and state

that I am the legal parent/guardian of _____

_____

who at this time is considered a minor, and is under the age
of eighteen years. I further state and grant permission for
___HYPNO-INVESTIGATOR___ representing ___AGENCY/___
___DEPARTMENT___ to conduct a hypnosis session and
administer hypnosis to the minor named above. I have read
and understand the procedure as explained to me and agree
to the hypnosis session and do hereby release and forever
hold harmless, ___DEPARTMENT/AGENCY___ , its agents,
employees, and/or anyone acting in its behalf, from any and
all claims, demands, or damages that may arise out of the
said examination and session.

PARENT/GUARDIAN: _____

WITNESS: _____

DATE: _____

INVESTIGATIVE HYPNOSIS
CONSENT & RELEASE FORM

STEP 2

CASE NO. _____

DATE: _____

TIME: _____

I _____ , do hereby voluntarily without objection, agree freely with full cooperation to undergo hypnosis, questioning and interview under hypnosis and further understand all interviews and sessions may be mechanically or video recorded as seen fit.

Permission is hereby granted for the hypnosis session as described above in order to assist the   RENO POLICE DEPT.   with an investigation currently in progress.

I also understand that I may be required to subsequently participate in this type of interview and hypnosis session for further verification purposes, to which I agree now and during the length of the ongoing investigation.

I further release and discharge   RENO POLICE DEPT.   , their agents and employees.

I further agree that the results of this session may be made available to the proper authorities, and I do hereby consent to everything that is necessary to be done and to be spoken in order to affect this request.

I have read the above and understand it completely.

SIGNED: _____

WITNESS: _____

(continued from preceding page)

PARENT/GUARDIAN CONSENT   *STEP 2*

I request that a hypnosis session be administered to:

_____, under the above
stated conditions. I further certify that I am the legal parent/
guardian of the above named person.

SIGNED:_____

WITNESS: _____

PRE-INDUCTION EXPLANATION NUMBER 1:

(Name), once you are in the state of hypnosis, you may doubt that you are in trance because of your heightened mental awareness. But, you will find that hypnosis is a process that enables you to relax better, hear better and to let what I say or what you think "sink in." This allows greater awareness. You are always in control. You will find it very comforting to just relax further and let things happen.

(Name), you can do anything in hypnosis that you can do out of it, and you will be able to do it much more effectively while in hypnosis because your awareness is so concentrated.

PRE-INDUCTION EXPLANATION NUMBER 2:

Hypnosis is a very useful tool which will allow you (name) to rid yourself of tension, anxiety and do many other marvelous things. Hypnosis especially allows you to relax. A person's mental alertness is heightened. You are never unconscious or in a natural sleep state. On the contrary, you will find that you are definitely more alert and have better clarity for images, things, and recollection. (Name), your senses are more acute. You will always have control over your actions and only do what you yourself believe and know that you want to do. In fact, the sounds around you may appear louder than usual. This is due to your hearing becoming a little more sensitive in the hypnotic state. As an individual lets himself go into hypnosis, various physical and physiological changes may begin to take effect. Some people tend to notice a change in their breathing. Their breathing may become softer, deeper and more gentle, and even more rhythmic. Other changes noticed are that a person's legs and arms sometimes become lighter and some people report a pleasant heaviness through-out their body. And, (name) while some of these physical changes are occurring, there are people that have said that their eyelids began to flutter or that they began to blink more than usual, and they found that when these things happened they began to relax more and could let themselves relax to a comfortable feeling very seldom experienced on an everyday level.

A person in hypnosis will always be able to return to a state of full awareness at any time they wish. Their mental awareness literally makes them acutely aware of all of their surroundings. (Name) when you let yourself go into that wonderful feeling of hypnosis you will be surprised that nothing will bother you in any way whatsoever. You will have a very relaxed attitude. And, if the door should open or an outside sound creeps through, you will find that you really will not be very concerned with it. And, the less concerned you become with any outside sounds, the more quickly they will fade into the distance. Nothing will ever be said to knowingly embarrass you nor will anything be done to cause you any discomfort. Now, (name) have you any questions about hypnosis that have not been explained, or that you would like answers to?

RESPONSIVE MENTAL EXERCISES (RME)   *STEP 4*

It was mentioned earlier that most (RME), "responsive mental exercises" can usually be adapted to hypnosis induction. It has been my experience to find that usually when a person is extremely frightened or possesses a fear of hypnosis, the conversion of a "responsive mental exercise" into hypnotic induction can be very time saving.

A suggested introduction to the (RME), "responsive mental exercise" can be as follows:
Now (Name), I would like you to cooperate with me for a little while and I would like you to work with me on some little "responsive mental exercises." This will give me an idea of how well we can work together or what types of induction methods I might use, in addition to seeing how well you understand my instructions. Let me show you how just by getting pictures in your mind and getting a mental image, we

are going to create a physical reaction in your body. Now (name), I'm going to show you how that works by having you close your eyes, extend your arms and hands straight out in front of you. Turn one palm up (subject's writing hand), and just follow along with me and listen to my voice. (OPERATOR MOVES INTO THE RME: ARMS LOWER/RAISED).

NUMBER 1: (RME) RESPONSIVE MENTAL EXERCISE: (ARMS LOWER/RAISED)

Now that you have your eyes closed and your arms out in front of you with your (right palm) facing up, I would like you to begin to use your imagination. And (name), I would like you to visualize and see in your imagination, your right hand holding a large book. It could be a dictionary or a large encyclopedia. And that book probably weighs about ten pounds. And (name), I would like you to see yourself standing there holding this book in your hand. You want to hand that book to someone, hand it to some people walking by, or maybe hand the book over to your friends. You see that big, heavy book in your hand as you wait for someone to take it from your hand. But, it seems no one is taking it from you. So, you are going to wait for a moment for someone to take that heavy book. Meanwhile while you are waiting for someone to take that heavy book from your hand, I want you to think and imagine that around your left wrist you have a string attached, and the string is leading up, up, up, and you can see that the string is tied to a big balloon. The balloon is your favorite color, and that big balloon is beginning to rise higher into the air, and as you look up at that balloon, it appears to be rising higher and higher. It seems like a light breeze is blowing that balloon higher and higher into the air. That big, beautiful balloon. Higher and higher. The balloon is continuing to drift toward the clouds, higher and higher and still higher. But (name), while that big balloon is climbing higher and higher, it seems that no one has come by yet to take that big, heavy book from your hand. So, while you are waiting for someone to take that heavy book from your hand, let's add another book weighing another ten pounds in your hand. Those two books feel so heavy, so very, very, heavy. Those books feel like the heaviest books you have ever held in your hand. And (name), if you draw your attention back to that favorite color balloon, you can see that it is still drifting higher and higher. That colorful balloon is drifting up, up, up, up toward the blue sky. And, that book is still getting heavier and heavier and heavier. So very, very, very, heavy. Now (name), if you will open your eyes. Open your eyes leaving your hands where they are. (IF RESPONSE WAS SUCCESSFUL) . . . The subject's arms will be at a great angle. The right hand very low and the left hand very high.

NUMBER 2:   (RME): HAND CLASP

What I would like you to do is to put your hands together. Now (name), interlock the fingers together. Lace your fingers together with the palms together and put your arms straight out in front of you, and continue to follow my instructions. With your hands out in front of you, I would like you to concentrate your attention on the crease in the palms of your hand. Right where the palms come together. Just keep your attention focused there on that spot and do not take your eyes off of that spot and continue to listen to my voice. And (name), as you do that I want you to begin putting a slight amount of pressure on the tips of your fingers. Begin to squeeze your fingers together. And (name), as you do that I would like you to put a little pressure on the palms of your hands. Squeezing the palms of your hands together, squeezing down, the palms of your hand, squeezing them down. Beginning to squeeze down, squeezing them down. And now, again I want you to use your imagination as you begin to squeeze down, and just for a moment, think that there is something in your hands that you just want to flatten, flatten out. Flatten it on down, that's it. I want you to put a

37

little more pressure, squeezing very tightly, very tightly now, squeezing tighter, tighter, and still tighter. Now, you can feel all the fingers melting together, being forged together and as that is happening, I am going to lock your fingers into place, very tightly into place. (OPERATOR LIGHTLY TOUCHES SUBJECT'S HANDS.) And, as I touch and lock your hands into place they are becoming tighter and tighter. Locking very tight. Locking very tight. (Name) your hands are locked so tight together that if you tried to pull them apart, you would find it very difficult to do so. Try, try and pull them apart and you will find that they are locked tight. The harder you try to pull your hands apart, the tighter they lock together. The more you try to separate your hands, the tighter they stick together. Stuck tight, STUCK TIGHT. Now on my signal, you will be able to unlock your hands. Relax now . . . and unlock your hands.

NUMBER 3:   (RME): SEESAW

I would like you to stand here. (OPERATOR INDICATES SPOT FOR SUBJECT TO STAND.) Now (name), put your toes together and your heels together. Let your arms drop loosely by your side. Close your eyes. Close your eyes and imagine that you are standing in the middle of a seesaw. A seesaw that you may have used when you were a child. And (name), while you are standing in the middle of the seesaw, there is a child at each end of the seesaw. As one child goes up, the other child goes down. And, you (name) go up and down, up and down, up and down, and as the children move faster, you go up and down faster and faster. Very good . . . you may open your eyes now and sit down before you fall down.

NUMBER 4:   (RME): GLUE ROUTINE

(OPERATOR INSTRUCTS THE SUBJECT TO EXTEND HIS FIRST FINGER AND THUMB. AND, PLACE ONE ON TOP OF THE OTHER.) Now that your thumb and finger are resting on each other, I would like you to do nothing but stare at the fingers while I am talking to you. While I talk to you, all you have to do is stare at the fingers resting on one another. Now (name), for the moment please move your finger out of the way and just stare at the thumb. Just slide the finger back away from the thumb and stare at the thumb while I talk to you.

Now, as you stare at the thumb I want you to use your imagination and think back when you were a child in school. I want you to think back when you were very young and when you took some water and flour and you made a little pasty glue. And, you used that pasty glue for sticking newspapers together and also used it to stick magazine clippings and cutouts together. Remember? Sometimes you got that pasty glue all over your fingers and sometimes you even got that pasty glue on your thumb. Sometimes you even got it all over your fingers and thumb. And, it got kind of messy. But (name) later on you went to another type of glue. It was brown, called LePage glue, and it had a big rubber nipple on the top of it. And, that glue was very good. You could put photographs in the family album. Maybe you clipped out pictures or recipes, or even pictures of your favority people or pets. And, while you were using this glue, remember how you got a lot of it all over your hands? Sometimes it even got stuck to your clothes. It was pretty good glue. But, then we came along with the white Elmer's glue, and on television you are shown that boards are glued together, and tractors then rip the boards apart, but the glued portion stays together. It is a strong glue, probably one of the strongest and stickiest. Then, along came the granddaddy of all glues. The stickiest, messiest strongest glue that ever came out. Perma bond glue. In fact, the perma bond glue is so strong that if you get a small amount on your skin, your skin sticks together. This perma bond glue is so powerful that you only get a very small amount, a tiny amount for a lot of money. But, it's so powerful, that it is worth the cost. Now (name) just imagine that powerful, sticky, strong glue, right there on your thumb. Now, put your finger down onto your thumb again. Put that finger right back into that glue on that thumb. Put that finger on that thumb stuck with glue until you feel your finger stuck tight to your thumb. As you place that finger on that thumb, your fingers will become stuck tight. Your fingers are stuck so tight together, you cannot get them apart. And, the harder you try to get your fingers apart the more that powerful glue is going to seal them tight together. Stuck tight, tight, tighter. STUCK TIGHT.

NUMBER 5:   (RME) FINGER CONTROL

Now that you have your eyes closed and feel relaxed I would like you to extend your hand (NOTE: OPERATOR DETERMINES IF SUBJECT IS RIGHT OR LEFT HANDED . . . . OPERATOR GIVES SUBJECT A PENCIL OR PEN TO PLACE BETWEEN THUMB AND FIRST FINGER.) Now (name) I want you to imagine that you have a string tied on each of those fingers holding that pencil. And, someone is now pulling on those strings and as the strings are being pulled . . . your fingers are slowly separating. Each pull on the string is pulling your fingers apart more and more away from that pencil. It feels as though you cannot hold onto that pencil anymore. Your fingers are being pulled apart by that string and the pencil is slipping, slipping from between your fingers.

At the Conclusion of
the (RME) "Responsive Mental Exercises"

You can explain: See, the moment you unquestionably accept what I tell you and you allow it to happen, *it will happen.* Just by getting these mental pictures in your mind, by using your imagination, the most powerful emotion that a person has, has allowed you to create a physical change in your body. Then is it not possible, that when you go into hypnosis and you let go, cooperate and use your imagination, you then can call on those parts of your subconscious mind to help you accomplish a better memory for your recollection, using me as a guide.

(NOTE: (RME): Responsive Mental Exercises are generally used to help determine the subject's suggestibility to hypnosis. With the aid of the information derived from the subject at the conclusion of the exercises, the hypno-investigator can gauge the ease or difficulty that the subject might display with regards to accepting hypnosis.)

There are many authors and hypnotists that give what is called: *Suggestibility Tests.* My coined phrase for the tecnnique is as stated: (RME). The reasoning behind that is one of words. The word *TEST* frightens many people. No matter what type of test. The person becomes frightened. They then feel they are going to have to produce specific results or they will *FAIL* the test. So, it is suggested that the hypno-investigator adopt my coined phrase of (RME): *Responsive Mental Exercises.* The subject would be more conducive to accepting working with you on a few *"mental exercises"* which does not indicate to him or her that they will have to pass or meet a general score situation. The cooperation will be much better and allow you, the hypno-investigator to judge the subject on the merits of the exercises. It should be added that if a subject does not perform one (RME) to the operator's satisfaction, the operator should pass on and go to another (RME), without any facial or verbal response indicating any lack of performance.

SUGGESTED HYPNOSIS INDUCTIONS   *STEP 5*

NOTE: All the inductions can be interchanged, and adapted to one another to suit the investigative hypnotist's needs. As always, if one induction method is not working to the hypno-investigator's satisfaction, SWITCH, interchange and combine various technics. The inductions are suggested for content

41

and the investigative hypnotist should adopt his most comfortable phraseology by the interchange of the various methods.

INDUCTION NUMBER 1: THE GIL BOYNE VARIATION ON THE DAVE ELMAN TWO FINGER TECHNIQUE

(Name), I would like you to place your feet flat on the floor and place your hands in your lap, let your hands hang very loose in your lap. Take a deep breath and hold it for a moment. Now, exhale and feel yourself relax. That's the idea . . . very loose and very comfortable. One more time if you will, inhale, hold it, hold it, now exhale very slowly, and as you exhale, just feel yourself relaxing even more. I would like you to keep your head level and as you keep your head perfectly level, I want you to focus your eyes on the edge of my hand. (OPERATOR'S HAND HELD ABOVE SUBJECT'S EYE LEVEL.) Now (name), keep your eyes focused on the edge of my hand and keep your head perfectly level and continue to listen to my voice. In a moment I am going to lower my hand. And, as I lower my hand down in front of your eyes, I want you to follow the edge of my hand with your eyes and allow your eyes to close down. And, at that point I want you to continue to follow my instructions. I am going to lower my hand down now and as I do I would like you to follow my hand down with your eyes, allow your eyes to close down and continue to follow my instructions. And, as your eyes close down, feel yourself relaxing down even more. Now that your eyes are closed down and closing even tighter as you gently press them together, I would like you to test your eyes and make sure they cannon open, test them, MAKE SURE THEY WILL NOT OPEN. And (name), the moment you realize that your eyes will not open, stop trying. Let the relaxation spread. Let that relaxation flow all the way down through your body. Let those eyes relax more. Let those eyebrows relax, relax, relax, that's it . . . . Let the relaxation flow all the way down through your body. Feel that relaxation moving through your arms and as it does, allow your arms to go limp and loose. Possibly your arms may even feel like two soft terry cloth towels. Loose, limp, and floppy. When I pick up your arms, they will relax even more and as I drop your arms into your lap, I want you to let that relaxation take you deeper, and relax even more. As the other arm is raised, you will feel yourself drifting even deeper and as that arm is gently dropped into your lap, feel yourself letting go and drifting even deeper. Let your body become totally relaxed. Every muscle and every fiber letting go. And (name) while you're relaxing even more, become aware of your breathing. You are now breathing very easily and very gently. In fact, you are going to relax still deeper and deeper with each and every breath you take. And, as you are drifting deeper with every breath, you will find yourself relaxing even more as I gently drop your arms from your lap to your sides. From this point on (name), nothing that I do or say will bother or disturb you in any way whatsoever. And, as I gently pick up your arms and let them fall gently back into your lap, you may feel all those muscles relaxing and every fiber letting go still more.

AT THIS POINT USE FURTHER
DEEPENING TECHNIQUES AS NEEDED.

INDUCTION NUMBER 2: DIRECT GAZE TECHNIQUE

(Name), I would like you to look directly into my eyes and listen to my instructions. In a moment I am going to count from one to ten, and as I count each number, I would like you to close your eyes down on the odd numbers and open them on the even numbers and each time you open your eyes, I want you to look directly into my eyes. (Name), as I continue to count the numbers toward the number ten, your eyes will become heavier and heavier, and more tired and you may feel like you will not want to open your eyes. However, by the time I reach the number ten, if your eyes are still open, I will just begin the count over again. If you must think of anything, just think of the fact that you are getting sleepy and drowsy. Now (name), on the count of 1, I would like you to close your eyes down. Begin to feel yourself relax even more now. (OPERATOR VARIES SPEED OF COUNT.) (OPERATOR PAUSES A LITTLE LONGER WHILE SUBJECT'S EYES ARE CLOSED ON ODD NUMBERS.) 2, 3 — As your eyes close on down, you can feel the relaxation deepen now. On the count of 4, 5, as your eyes drift down, you can feel your eyes becoming heavier and heavier, very heavy and very tired. 6, 7, you can feel yourself drifting down even deeper now. Feel the relaxation spreading deeper and deeper and the eyelids getting heavier and heavier, so very heavy. On the count of 8, 9, your eyelids begin closing down, and as your eyelids close down, you feel more calm, more relaxed, more rested and the eyes themselves seem to be getting heavier and heavier. 10, 1 closing down, feeling so heavy and so tired now. Feel your head beginning to drift toward your chest and as it does you begin to relax even more. Feel yourself drifting still deeper and deeper and relaxed in a comfortable state. Now that you are so deeply and comfortably relaxed . . . .

OPERATOR THEN PROCEEDS WITH ADDITIONAL DEEPENING TECHNIQUES AS NEEDED. IF SUBJECT STILL IS OPENING EYES AFTER OPERATOR GETS TO THE NUMBER TEN, THE OPERATOR JUST BEGINS THE COUNT OVER AGAIN, BEFORE PROCEEDING WITH ADDITIONAL DEEPENING.

INDUCTION NUMBER 3: FINGER-HAND FIXATION

(OPERATOR INSTRUCTS SUBJECT TO PLACE HAND IN LAP, PALM UP.) What I would like you to do is let your hand rest loose and limp in your lap and as it does I would like you to concentrate your attention on that finger.

(OPERATOR INDICATES FINGER.) Do not take your eyes off of that finger. And (name), as you continue to watch that finger, you will soon notice that the other fingers will begin to relax. In fact, each finger will relax and each finger will begin to separate as they relax. The fingers will separate as if little wedges have been driven between each finger. There they go now . . . there goes the little finger, it's beginning to move. Now your concentration can be expanded to all of the fingers on that hand. Next the ring finger is moving and now the middle finger. And as the fingers begin to separate slowly at first, they appear to be moving apart a little faster now. All of those fingers are spreading apart and separating. Wider and wider and wider. Now (name), you can see big spaces between all of those fingers . . . that's it, there they go, wider and wider, as the fingers relax still further. And as the fingers relax more and more, so does your body relax more and more. Just like little wedges being driven between those fingers, opening them wider and wider, and letting you relax still more and more. Now, you will notice that those fingers seem to have a will of their own. Your hand is now feeling very light and those fingers will soon begin to move toward your eyebrows and face. Those fingers will move directly toward your face and as you watch that hand it will at first move slowly, steadily, directly toward your face and eyebrows. Or even perhaps toward the tip of your nose or your cheek. As you keep your attention focused on that hand and fingers, the hand is moving closer and closer. And, as the hand moves closer to your face you are going to notice that you are staring and therefore you have a slight bit of eyestrain. And as you strain your eyes, they will begin to get heavier than they are now. Heavy and tired. You may find that you may even want to blink your eyes and clear your vision. You may even see eight fingers instead of four fingers. But (name), as you watch, the eyes will blink down and become heavier and heavier, more tired, drowsier, and dreamier. Now, let your eyes close and as your eyes close, your hand

45

will continue to move toward your face and, when your hand touches your face in any way, you will drift into a sound, deep form of hypnotic trance.

PROCEED WITH ADDITIONAL
DEEPENING TECHNIQUES AS NEEDED

INDUCTION NUMBER 4:   HAND BODY FIXATION

Now (name), place both of your feet flat on the floor and put one hand on each leg. Feet flat on the floor, one hand on each leg. Now, watch one of your hands. Take whichever hand is more convenient, and watch that hand. From this point on, do not remove your eyes from that hand. Pay attention to nothing but that hand and the sound of my voice. Listen to nothing but my voice. Watch your hand and listen to nothing but my voice and soon a very pleasant drowsiness will come about. Soon your eyelids may become heavy. Your eyes may appear to burn or sting or possibly they will water. Do not deliberately close your eyes. Do not make any effort to keep them open. Just constantly watch that hand and experience everything that you can about that hand. And (name), as you watch that hand, any thoughts that come about other than relaxation, let them pass. Any sounds about the room or from outside, other than my voice, let those sounds drift into the background. Listen to nothing but my voice, think of nothing but relaxation. Soon much of your body may seem heavy, while other parts of your body may seem lighter than some. Begin to breathe deeply (name). Take a deep breath. Breathing deeply helps you relax even more. Fill your lungs up, and let it out slowly. Let it out slowly and relax as you exhale. Just let every muscle in your body totally relax. Deep breath, and then let it out slowly, relaxing a little more each time that you exhale. So (name), constantly breathe deeply and regularly, breathe deeply, relax as you exhale. Just let every muscle in your body relax. Notice now, you watch that hand as you breathe deeply. Let your facial muscles begin to relax. Begin by relaxing the area around your eyes. Relax the areas around your eyes. Your cheeks and jaws. Open your mouth slightly, this will make it easier to breathe as we go along. Constantly breathe deeply and regularly (name). Constantly breathe deeply, regularly and relax. Constantly breathe deeply and regularly and relax as you exhale. Concentrate your thoughts on those areas I mentioned, and allow those areas to relax. Relax totally. Concentrate on those areas. (Name), let your scalp relax, let your scalp and face relax. Now your neck, your neck and now your shoulders. Let this relaxation flow through your body. Let every muscle, every nerve and every fiber in your body totally relax. Relax your scalp and your face, relax your scalp and your face, your neck. Your neck and your shoulders. Now your arms. Your arms and your hands, and all your fingers. Relax. Just let yourself melt into that chair as you relax still more. Any time I touch you this will only help you relax. This will only be to help you relax and send you even deeper. Just let go. (OPERATOR LIGHTLY AND GENTLY TOUCHES SUBJECT ON THE SHOULDER.) Let go and totally relax. Relax your scalp and your face. Your scalp, your face and your neck. Your neck and shoulders. Your arms and now your hands. Relax your arms and your hands and let all of your fingers relax. Just let yourself melt into that chair, and completely, totally, relax. Relax your scalp and your face, relax your scalp and your face, your neck, your shoulders, your arms and your hands. And, let all of your fingers relax. Now relax your back. Let this relaxation move through your spine down into your hips. Relax your back and now your chest. Let go. Let every single muscle simply relax. Relax your back and your chest. Your back and your chest and now your stomach. Your stomach, now your waist, now your hips. Just let go. Let yourself go. Completely and totally relaxed. Relax your stomach and your waist, your stomach and your waist. Now your hips. Just let go. Don't be tense. Let every muscle totally relax. Relax your stomach and your waist, your hips, your hips and now your thighs. Relax your waist and hips, your waist and hips and thighs. Your thighs and now your knees, your knees and now your calves. Every muscle in your entire body totally relaxed. Relax your knees and your calves. Your knees and your calves and now your ankles. Your ankles and now your feet. Relax your ankles and your feet. Relax your ankles and your feet. Just let go. Let every muscle completely relax. Just let yourself go, (name), and relax. Deep breath, fill up your lungs, hold it, hold it, let it out slowly, slowly, relaxing more and more, as you go way down deeper, deeper and deeper into this wonderful, wonderful state of relaxation. Every muscle in your body completely and totally relaxed. Now, let's do that one more time, (name). Deep breath, deeper, deeper. And, let it out slowly, slowly relaxing more and more. Going deeper and deeper. Every muscle in your body completely relaxed, totally relaxed. Now (name), let's go through that progressive relaxation just one more time to insure that you relax even more. (OPERATOR STEPS UP PACE OF INDUCTION.) Relax your scalp. Relax your scalp and face. Relax your scalp, your face and your neck. Your neck and now your shoulders (OPERATOR GENTLY TOUCHES SUBJECT ON THE SHOULDER.) Just let go, (name). Let every muscle totally relax. Relax your neck and your shoulders. Your neck and your shoulders, and now your arms. Your arms and now your hands. Just let yourself go. Let every muscle totally relax. Relax your neck and shoulders. Your neck and your shoulders, now your arms. Your arms and now your hands. Let your neck and your shoulders, your arms, your arms and your hands relax. And, let your fingers relax. Now relax your back and your chest. Totally relax. Relax your back and your chest and your stomach. Your stomach and now your waist. Relax your stomach, your waist, your hips. Your hips and now your thighs. Relax your waist, your hips and your thighs. Your thighs and now your knees relax, (name). Just let go even further and relax. Relax your knees and your calves, your ankles. Your ankles and your feet. Let all of your toes relax, let all of your toes relax. You are more relaxed now than you ever imagined. And, (name), you are going to relax even more as we go along.

PROCEED WITH DEEPENING TECHNIQUE
AS NEEDED

INDUCTION NUMBER 5:   SPIRAL EYE FIXATION

(Name), please keep your eyes directly on that spiral if you will and as you watch the center of it you will notice that as it goes around and around, it seems to have a very soothing and relaxing effect. And, (name), as you keep your attention focused deep into the center of it, you may find that it goes out of focus, it may blur, blur a little bit. If it does, do not try to correct your vision, (name). Just try to look at it in a very lazy sort of way, a relaxed manner. And, as you do, you will notice that it begins to form a tunnel. As it forms a tunnel, it seems like it is drawing you inside. Deep down inside of that tunnel. And, (name), just keep your eyes on the spiral as it slowly softens, and turns, and spirals. It seems as though it is pulling you down, down, down and down. And, (name), you keep your eyes open just as long as you possibly can. As you watch it, it may feel as though your eyes are getting a little drowsy, a little dreamy. You may even feel your eyes tear a little. Or, you may feel your eyes getting very heavy, very tired, and you may want to close your eyes. But, (name), just keep looking at the spiral and watch it soften, and flow, as it goes around and around, seeming to come closer and closer. It seems to be beckoning you inward as if you feel as though you just want to float into the center of that spiral. As the spiral goes around and around, you can feel your eyes begin to flutter, beginning to get very, very, heavy, tired, dreamy, drowsy. And, as you continue to watch the spiral, especially notice the center of the spiral. As you do, your eyes will get heavier and heavier and more tired and dreamy. It seems as though you forgot all those things around you that have been outside noises, as if nothing around you bothers you or disturbs you in any way. As you continue to listen to my voice and watch the center of the spiral, you can feel yourself drifting even deeper into the center and still becoming drowsier and dreamier. As you watch it, your eyes will get so heavy and so tired that you will not want to keep them open. Soon, you will just want to let your eyes close down as you continue to watch the spinning and spinning around, soft spiraling around and around, drawing you down and down and down. You can now feel your eyes getting so heavy and so tired that you begin to feel your eyelids fluttering even more and it becomes very difficult now to keep the eyes open. It seems as though it is all blurring together. It's very hard to make the spiral out as it draws you down. And, as it does, your eyes are so heavy, so heavy and so tired, they are closing down now. You do not feel like you really want to watch the spiral anymore. The eyes are getting heavier and heavier and more tired. Drowsier and dreamier. Just allow your eyes to close down and as your eyes close down, you will continue to see the spiral going around and around under your eyelids. Making you even dreamier and drowsier than you are right now. Relaxing you even more and taking you still deeper into a very comfortable, serene, relaxed state. Drifting, drifting down so that nothing bothers you, nothing disturbs you, nothing awakens you, until I give you the signal to awaken. This relaxed, serene feeling is spreading very rapidly throughout your entire body, (name). And now, (name), with your eyes tightly closed, the relaxation begins to spread to all those muscles throughout your body.

OPERATOR CAN CONTINUE WITH PROGRESSIVE RELAXATION OR PROCEED TO DEEPENING AS NEEDED

INDUCTION NUMBER 6: CONFUSION INDUCTION

Sometimes it is pleasant to sit (lay) back and relax, to let your muscles go loose and limp and to let go. (Name), as you listen to me and concentrate on what I am saying, a spontaneous and automatic relaxation will take place. At times you can be aware of certain things and at other times, you may not be aware of them. For instance, you might be aware of a picture on the wall if you look at it. You might be looking at it, but if your attention is elsewhere, as on possibly that lamp, or window over there, you might not be aware of that picture. However, (name), you might be aware of it subconsciously even if you are not looking at it. Right now, there is something you are unaware of until I mention it to you. And when I do, you will become aware of it, very much aware of it. That is having shoes on your feet. Now you can feel them, and you can be aware of me and what I am saying to you or may say to you, or might have said, or you may not be aware of some things that I say, but your subconscious could very well be aware of them. You can also be aware of time or unaware of it. You can be aware of the present, or the past, or the future. You can even remember various things about the present, the past, or the future when that becomes the past. Day before yesterday, yesterday was tomorrow and that was the future. And then, yesterday became today and was the past. And (name), tomorrow will soon be today and then yesterday or tomorrow can become today, or even the day after tomorrow. You may even remember last January first when you wrote 1980 when it was really 1981. It may be interesting for you as you sit (lie) here to recall that the time is (whatever hour it is). And, as you sit and think about the time, it is interesting to realize that today is (give date). Yesterday at this hour, you probably were doing something else. Perhaps you were relaxed as you are now. And, you may be reminded today of how relaxed you were. Just so relaxed. Or you may have been home, or at your business, or even someplace else. You may even be reminded today of just how relaxed you were that day. And, maybe, you might have been listless and drowsy and sleepy, really relaxed. How pleasant it was to relax completely and let go and forget about today. You may have even found your eyes closing as you relaxed. You were very comfortable and it is always good to relax and let all your muscles go loose and limp, and you can remember times when you were very sleepy. Also remembering how pleasant it is to drift off and relax and sleep. Sleeping deeply, deeply and soundly. And (name), you can probably feel those feelings growing stronger and can relax completely now.

ADDITIONAL RELAXATION TECHNIQUE OR
DEEPENING TECHNIQUE AS REQUIRED

INDUCTION NUMBER 7: ANALYTICAL

(Name), as you comfortably sit in that chair with your eyes beginning to tire, listening to my instructions, you may begin to think that you want to resist nodding off to sleep. You may have many thoughts going through your mind at this time. One main thought might be that, "I am here listening to that person's voice. I cannot fall into a sleep." But, (name), you will begin to find that the more you fight the feeling of relaxation, calm, serenity and sleep, the more difficult it will be to actually keep your eyes open. Because as you have been brought up to realize, when a person closes their eyes, and they keep their eyes closed, sleep can actually be accomplished. So, (name), the harder and stronger you actually fight and resist closing your eyes and relaxing completely, the more relaxed you will begin to feel. In fact, the stronger you resist the sleepier you will become. (Name), resist very hard when you feel your eyes want to close. Because you will find the harder you try, the more relaxed, serene and comfortable you are going to become. Really try very hard to stay awake. Stay awake and try not to listen to my voice. While you sit there becoming more relaxed, comfortable, calm and serene, trying not to pay attention to what I am saying, you will find yourself becoming more relaxed, sleepy and cooperative the harder you try not to sleep, and pay attention to my voice. Try not to relax and sleep (name), the harder you try the more relaxed and sleepier you get. In fact your eyelids are getting very, very heavy. Heavier and heavier until they close (name).

PROCEED WITH DEEPENING TECHNIQUE
AS NEEDED

CHALLENGE SUGGESTIONS *STEP 6*

CHALLENGE SUGGESTIONS begin usually with the easiest for the subject to perform and progressively increase to the more difficult. In addition to the various depth scales mentioned in this handbook, a description of basic challenges is provided for your informational use.

(Also see the various hypnotic scales in supplemental section in back of the book.)

CHALLENGE NUMBER 1: EYE CATALEPSY

Relax all the muscles around your eyes. Your eyes are closed tight. If you tried to open your eyes, it would be very difficult. All the muscles around your eyes seem so relaxed, so loose and so limp that you cannot open your eyes. Make sure your eyes will not open, try to open them. The harder you try, the tighter closed they stay. They are locked tight shut. Now (name), STOP TRYING, just relax and go deeper relaxed, into that wonderful hypnotic state.

RECOMMENDED TIME TO ALLOW
SUBJECT TO OPEN EYES IS APPROXIMATELY
3 OR 4 SECONDS ON FIRST CHALLENGE.

**CHALLENGE NUMBER 2: ARM CATALEPSY OR
                       LEG CATALEPSY**

ARM CATALEPSY: (OPERATOR EXTENDS THE SUB-
JECT'S ARM AND TELLS SUBJECT THAT HIS ARM IS
BECOMING VERY STIFF, STIFF AND RIGID. JUST AS
STIFF AND RIGID AS A STEEL BAR.) It is solid, stiff, and
rigid. When I touch your arm again, you will find that the
more you try to bend your arm, the stiffer it becomes. Now,
try to bend it and you find it growing stiffer and stiffer. Now
(name), stop trying, and let yourself relax still deeper into the
wonderful hypnotic state.

LEG CATALEPSY: (SAME AS ABOVE WITH SLIGHT
VARIATION:) You will find that your legs are so stiff, so stiff
and rigid and heavy, the more you try to move them the
heavier they become. Stiff, rigid and heavy. Now (name),
STOP TRYING and let yourself drift still deeper into that
comfortable, relaxed state of hypnosis.

DEEPENING TECHNIQUES   *STEP* 7

DEEPENING procedures vary from individual to individual.
I find that a subject can be deepened sufficiently while in a
light state of hypnosis. However it is my personal feeling
which is based on actual experience that the subject should
be deepened to the deepest level possible. Somnambulistic, if
possible. I have found from experience that more can be accomplished, the deeper the subject is in hypnosis.

**DEEPENING PROCEDURE
NUMBER 1:   COUNTING**

I am going to allow you a few moments of relaxation (name).
You will relax even deeper with every breath you take. In a
moment I am going to count slowly backwards from ten to
zero. And, as I count backwards, I want you to let your body

relax more and more with each count. In fact, at the count of five, you will be even more relaxed than ever before, then you will go still deeper as each number becomes smaller and smaller. Counting now . . . 10, completely relaxed all over now (name). Your body is growing heavier and tired, you're going down deeper and deeper to sleep. 9, all those worldly things seem so far away and remote now as you drift still deeper and deeper into the most relaxed sleep ever known to man. It's a restful, calm, serene sleep. A peaceful comfortable sleep. 8, a wonderful sleep, a dreamless sleep. 7, you're completely relaxed all over now. You can begin to feel all the tensions of the day and all of that muscular tension disappearing now. 6, you can feel everything letting go at once now. Deeper and deeper and deeper. In just a moment you are going off into the best, restful, sleep ever known. 5, you're more relaxed now than ever before. 4, now you can feel everything letting go in your body. Letting go all at once. You can even feel the weight of your body. It may feel heavy or may even feel light in those certain parts. You feel so tired. 3, you are going down still further into that restful sleep I described to you. It is peaceful, serene, calm, and you're going still deeper to sleep from this point on. Every word I say will only carry you deeper to sleep until I give you the signal to awaken. Every breath you take will carry you deeper into this wonderful state. 2, so deep now that only sleep seems to matter. So deep that only the sound of my voice is important for you to even relax more. 1, drifting still ever deeper and deeper. Zero, you are now going deeper and deeper, you are in a wonderful state of hypnotic sleep and drifting deeper with each and every breath you take.

ADDITIONAL DEEPENING OR PROCEED TO
INSTILL INSTANT SLEEP SUGGESTION (I.S.S.)

DEEPENING PROCEDURE
NUMBER 2:   VERBAL DEPTH

As you feel yourself very dreamy, very drowsy, drifting deeper and deeper, you will relax even more. It totally, thoroughly relaxes you, drifting down, deeper, deeper, deeper and still deeper in the relaxed, comfortable state. You may find that your head will become very heavy and very tired. Your head may even have a tendency to drift toward your chest. And, if it does (name), allow it to do so. You may find that your entire body wants to relax and as that happens you will breathe even slower and deeper and relax still more. If this happens, allow it to happen. Feel yourself drifting down to a very comfortable state and very relaxed feeling. Drifting deeper and still deeper as each moment passes by. And (name), from this moment on, each and every breath you take is going to relax you more and carry you deeper and still deeper into a very sound hypnotic sleep. A deep sleep, a sound sleep, where nothing will bother or disturb you, or awaken you, until I give you the signal to awaken.

ADDITIONAL DEEPENING OR PROCEED TO
(I.S.S.) INSTANT SLEEP SUGGESTION

DEEPENING PROCEDURE   ELEVATOR
NUMBER 3:   IMAGERY

Now (name), I would like you to use your imagination. I would like you to imagine that you are on the tenth floor of a building. Any building, either real or imaginary. And (name), I want you to visualize and see yourself walking toward the bank of elevators in the building. Now the images are becoming more vivid. See yourself reach out, you press the button calling for the elevator car. And, you wait a moment. You hear the little ring of the bell signaling the car has arrived. See the doors as they slide gently open. Now you can walk into the elevator, turn your back to the wall and face the doors.

As you face the doors, you raise your eyes and look directly above the doors and notice the number 10 is lit, and glowing. You are on the tenth floor. You can hear the hum of the machinery as the door glides closed. You can begin to feel the elevator drift down toward the ground floor, and as it drifts down, it is going to carry you into a much deeper and deeper state of hypnosis and relaxation than you are in now. You watch the number 10 and as the number 10 blinks out you feel the elevator drifting down. And, the number 9 comes on, and as you pass the ninth floor and the number 9 blinks out, you drift still deeper into hypnosis and relaxation, becoming more dreamy and drowsy. You can see the number 8 come on. It glows brightly, the number 8. As you pass the eighth floor, the 8 blinks out and the number 7 lights up and as it does, you can feel yourself drifting deeper, and deeper. Now, you watch the 7 go out and the number 6 lights up. As you pass the sixth floor, you drift still deeper and feel total relaxation flowing through your entire body. The fifth floor, now even deeper. Now the fourth floor, still deeper, and deeper. The third floor, and going ever so deep. (OPERATOR SPEAKS SOFTER.) Second floor, drifting even deeper and deeper, first floor, and still deeper. And now (name), the ground floor, totally relaxed, feeling serene, calm, comfortable, and DEEP ASLEEP.

ADDITIONAL DEEPENING OR PROCEED TO
(I.S.S.) INSTANT SLEEP SUGGESTION

DEEPENING PROCEDURE
NUMBER 4:   **STAIRCASE**

You are standing at the top of a flight of stairs. As you are standing there looking down, holding on securely to the hand rail, you notice there are ten stairs. As you step down each step to get to the bottom of the staircase, you will drift deeper and deeper with each step. As you step from the tenth step to the ninth, you can feel yourself becoming still more relaxed. Even more than before. From the ninth to the eighth, feel yourself going deeper and deeper, eight to seven, and still deeper. Seven to the sixth step, and letting go to that feeling of total relaxation. Five, relaxing even more than before, fourth step, third step and drifting deeper, becoming more relaxed, calm, and loose and limp. Second step, drifting deep, deep, deeper. And finally, the first step. You feel so tired, so drowsy, so dreamy that you just want to sit on that first step for a moment. And (name), as you do, you can and will feel yourself relaxing still deeper than you have relaxed before. You can feel yourself relaxing so deep, so, so deep, that you just want to drift deeper. Drifting down. It is such a good feeling, such a comfortable feeling, such a relaxing feeling. From this moment on, every breath you take will carry you still deeper and more and more relaxed into a very deep sleep, a very sound sleep.

ADDITIONAL DEEPENING AS NEEDED OR PROCEED TO (I.S.S.) INSTANT SLEEP SUGGESTION

DEEPENING PROCEDURE NUMBER 5:   **HAMMOCK IMAGERY**

I would like you to use your imagination. I want you to use your imagination and visualize yourself lying in a hammock. Picture yourself lying in a hammock on a pleasant day beneath the trees. It is a pleasant day and you're so very relaxed. Just let yourself go. Relax more and more. A pleasant breeze is swaying the trees back and forth. You're looking at the sky through the limbs of the trees. The trees are swaying back and forth and you're relaxing more and more as the trees sway back and forth. I am going to count from ten to zero and you are going to actually feel as though your hammock is drifting back and forth, back and forth with each count. And (name), when I reach zero, you will be completely in a state of hypnosis and relaxation.

FURTHER DEEPENING OR (I.S.S.)

DEEPENING PROCEDURE NUMBER 6:   **HAND AND ARM DROP TECHNIQUE**

Now (name), I am going to gently pick up your hand and just drop in into your lap. I want to feel all the weight in the hand. I do not want you to help me in any way. As I drop the hand down into your lap, I want you to let yourself go and deepen your relaxation. Now (name), as I pick up the other hand, hold it for a moment you will feel yourself going deeper. And, as I gently drop it into your lap, I want you to relax even more, and go even deeper than you are now into the relaxation of hypnosis. Now, I am going to drop both of your hands from your lap and they will fall loosely to your sides. As I do that you will let yourself go completely and go still deeper than you are now. Very deeply, very soundly, into the hypnotic sleep. In a moment, I am going to raise and drop your hands back into your lap. Nothing that I do will bother or disturb you. Any physical touch by me will only help you go deeper and deeper into this wonderful state. You will be aware that I am raising and dropping your hands and each and every time I gently drop your hands, you will feel yourself letting go, relaxing more and more.

ADDITIONAL DEEPENING TECHNIQUES OR PROCEED TO (I.S.S.) INSTANT SLEEP SUGGESTION

DEEPENING PROCEDURE NUMBER 7:   **FRACTIONATION TECHNIQUE**

While you are in this safe, secure, comfortable position, relaxed and drifting deeper, you will find yourself drifting deeper with each and every breath you take from this point on. And (name), as you continue to drift deeper into the relaxed state, you will continue to listen to the sound of my voice and when I instruct you to open your eyes as I count to three, you will open your eyes, feeling very relaxed, sleepy and very anxious to return to the comfortable hypnotic, relaxed state. When I count three the second time, you will very easily drop off into that relaxed state of hypnosis once again even deeper than before. Then (name), thereafter as I count to three you will open your eyes, and feel sleepier than the time before and as I repeat the count of three, you will very easily and quickly drop back into that very wonderful, relaxed, calm, sleep that relaxed hypnotic state even deeper than the time before.

ADDITIONAL DEEPENING TECHNIQUE AS NEEDED OR PROCEED WITH (I.S.S.) INSTANT SLEEP SUGGESTION

DEEPENING PROCEDURE NUMBER 8: **IMAGERY TECHNIQUES**

The subject is asked to imagine trips through forests, walks on the beach, walks or trips through the forests and hills, lakes, etc. Basically any scene that is relaxing to the subject can be described. All the while the operator should incorporate all of the subject's senses into the image scene. The touch, taste, smell, feel, hear standard should apply when permissible.

DEEPENING PROCEDURE NUMBER 9: **ANOTHER VERBAL SUGGESTION**

(Name), I want you to continue to drift still deeper than you are now. Feel yourself going very limp and continuing to do so. Feel yourself becoming pleasantly warm and comfortable. The same pleasant warm and comfortable feeling you may get lying in your own bed at home. Feel those covers and blankets pulled around you for that warm, comforting, relaxing feeling. It feels so soft, so warm, so comfortable. A very pleasing soft, warm, comfort. Drifting deeper and deeper into a comfortable and relaxed sleep. So deep asleep that you will not want to open your eyes until I ask you to do so. Drifting deeper with each sound of my voice. Remember, you will always be able to hear everything that I say to you and you will always understand each and every word I say to you. Nothing will bother or disturb you as you let go and drift deeper and deeper into hypnosis.

ADDITIONAL DEEPENING AS NEEDED OR PROCEED TO (I.S.S.) INSTANT SLEEP SUGGESTION

(I.S.S.) INSTANT SLEEP SUGGESTIONS   *STEP 8*

Basically the instant sleep suggestion is found on the post-hypnotic suggestion. When the subject responds to an I.S.S. it can be assumed that the subject is conditioned and at an adequate depth for most suggestions by the hypno-investigator. The I.S.S. acts as a catalyst to rehypnotize without a lengthy procedure. It is especially useful when the subject becomes emotional and abreacts during revivification.

(I.S.S.) NUMBER 1:

(Name), every time I place my hand on your shoulder, and say the word "sleep," in this manner (OPERATOR TOUCHES SUBJECT ON SHOULDER VERY GENTLY AND SAYS THE WORD "SLEEP") you will stop whatever you were saying or doing, close your eyes, and drift back into a state of sleep even deeper than the one you are now in. Yes, (name), each and every time I suggest sleep and touch you on the shoulder, you will sleep very quickly, deeply, and very soundly. Each time drifting deeper and deeper.

(I.S.S.) NUMBER 2:

Each and every time I suggest sleep to you and touch your

hand in this manner, you will automatically sleep deeply and soundly. Even deeper than you are now.

SUGGESTIONS, WHEN HYPNO-INVESTIGATOR TAKES HYPNOTIC CONTROL
FOR INFORMATION RETRIEVAL   *STEP 9*

The suggestions that the investigative hypnotist administers to the subject are tailored to the issue at hand under investigation. However, this section will offer a selection of suggestions that may assist the hypno-investigator formulate their line of pursuit pertaining to the investigation at issue. It has been this writer's experience that the format using the information supplied herein proved very beneficial for information retrieval.

INVESTIGATIVE   TELEVISION
SUGGESTION NUMBER 1:   TECHNIQUE

Now (name), I would like you to visualize yourself sitting in your favorite chair to watch television. You're going to see a very special program. The program and film can slow down, stop, speed up, and operate on close-ups, on both scenes and people. Thus, enabling you (name), to see more clearly, all those certain things that your mind knows you actually saw.

INVESTIGATIVE
SUGGESTION NUMBER 2:   MIRROR TECHNIQUE
Developed by Dr. Bradley Kuhns

(Name), I now want you to recall the events of (matter at issue), (date, place, etc.). And (name), you will find that you will be able to disclose the events and developments that took place, very easily, clearly, and vividly. Now (name), I would like you to use your imagination and visualize a mirror. A mirror that you are familiar with. The mirror may or may not be full length or it could even be one that you yourself use every day. And, (name), after you are visualizing the mirror clearly, I want you to signal me by raising this finger (OPERATOR TOUCHES SUBJECT'S RIGHT OR LEFT INDEX FINGER). (AFTER FINGER RAISES), That's fine (name), now as you have seen many times in the movies or on t.v., a person can gaze into a mirror and see things that happened at an earlier time, just by looking at the incident in the mirror. And now, (name), you will be able to look into that mirror, and by this means, you will be able to describe everything that happened: (matter at issue) (incident), in a correct chronological sequence just by watching that mirror, which is very, very clear. In fact, nothing is more clear than a mirror image. In turn, this will allow you to see everything that occurred very clearly. (Name), after you awaken, you will have no loss of memory or recall to any recollections whatsoever. You will notice that you will be able to remember all of the details, even though some may return to you slowly. Remember (name), whatever you view in that mirror will be very, very clear, very vivid and concise and accurate as you actually saw, heard or felt the situation.

INVESTIGATIVE
SUGGESTION NUMBER 3:

POST-HYPNOTIC
SUGGESTION

(Name), you find it very easy to remember that matter (concerning the automobile accident) without too much effort tomorrow. Even though it seems to be a bit hazy at this time. In fact (exact time) i.e. (2 p.m.) tomorrow, which is a definite time will be approximately the time you have a clear and vivid recollection of (matter at issue) i.e. (automobile accident).

INVESTIGATIVE
SUGGESTION NUMBER 4:

POST-HYPNOTIC
SUGGESTION

Recalling incident when (subject has difficulty)

(Name), you will be hypnotized again tomorrow, and at

that time you automatically remember the (correct license plate) number or (whatever material the hypno-investigator) is seeking. In the next two or three days (name), after completion of your hypnosis session, should you recall, recollect or remember anything whatsoever about this (crime, investigation, whatever), you have a strong urge to call, and call the investigators handling the matter. You relate your recall and recollection to them. And (name), you do this even though the material may seem insignificant to you.

INVESTIGATIVE SUGGESTION NUMBER 5: POST HYPNOTIC SUGGESTION

(Name), when you awaken from this very relaxed state of hypnosis you very easily relate that which you related under this state of hypnosis and relaxation. In other words (name), you recount the same thing that you recounted under hypnosis. You find that you will be able to remember everything just as you described and told it to me. When you awaken you have an extremely clear and vivid recollection and recall of everything you have told me.

INVESTIGATIVE SUGGESTION NUMBER 6: IDEO-MOTOR RESPONSE FORMAT

Ideo-motor response explanation = Briefly the ideo-motor activity refers to the involuntary capacity of a subject's muscles to respond instantaneously to thoughts, feelings and ideas.

(Name), the forefingers and thumbs of your right and left hands are now under direct control of your subconscious mind. And (name), I will guide and direct your subconscious mind to reply to questions by lifting your (right forefinger) to indicate "yes" . . . the (left forefinger) to indicate "no," the (right thumb) to give the signal "I don't know" and the (left thumb) to indicate "I don't want to answer."

Author's note: Always caution for the protection and safety of bringing to the surface any repressed or traumatic materials. (i.e.) (name), is it alright for you to remember (whatever the incident)? If the hypno-investigator receives a negative answer, no attempt should be made to delve and retrieve the materials at that time.

| INVESTIGATIVE SUGGESTION NUMBER 7: | POST HYPNOTIC (HYPNOTIC LIE DETECTION TECHNIQUE) |

It should be noted that there are many methods depicting the use of hypnosis and various lie detection techniques. One of the approaches of this writer in using a lie detection technique is best described as: (name), I would like you to notice that your left hand is becoming very itchy, especially in this specific area. (Hypno-investigator touches area to itch) (i.e., top of subject's left hand, behind the middle finger). Your left hand in this area is becoming very itchy, the itch is centered in this area (touch area). Now (name), to make the itch go away, all you have to do is scratch the itch with *"ONLY"* the fingers of your right hand. Now (name), make the itch go away. Scratch that itch with the fingers of your right hand . . . . That's it . . . that s fine.

Now (name), from this point on that itch will only return whenever you actually lie to me about something. And (name), each and every time you do actually lie to me about something, you will unconsciously scratch that itch with your *FINGERS* of your right hand. (Name), remember also, that a lie is a lie. A little lie is the same as a big lie. So (name), whenever you lie to me in any way whatsoever, the itch will occur on your left hand, specifically where I touched it, very strongly. Just like an itch from an insect bite, stinging and very itchy. And (name), the only thing that will stop that itch is your scratching it with only the fingers of your right hand. (HYPNO-INVESTIGATOR CONDITIONS SUBJECT

TO REACTION.) (WATCH RESPONSE FOR EXACTNESS, SPECIFIC AREA, ONLY FINGERS.) After you awaken (name), you will have no recollection, recall or even remember that we discussed this matter of lying. However (name), after you awaken, any time you actually or intentionally lie to me, those automatic reactions on your part will happen. And (name), each response will happen quickly, swiftly and automatically. (THEN QUESTION THE SUBJECT IN THE WAKING STATE.)

RETURN AND REMOVE
(WAKE UP)   *STEP 10*

Prior to bringing a subject out of hypnosis, all unwanted suggestions should be removed. Once the unwanted suggestions are removed the hypno-investigator can proceed with the wake up procedure.

WAKE UP PROCEDURE NUMBER 1:

(Name), I am going to count from one to ten. As I count each number you will awaken slowly with each count. You will become more refreshed, relaxed and rested with each count and on the count of eight you will open your eyes, on nine you will be wide awake and on ten you will be totally wide awake.

WAKE UP PROCEDURE NUMBER 2:

One, you are beginning to awaken, two, you are completely relaxed and rested, three, you are physically refreshed and very mentally alert. Four, you are exceptionally clear headed, wonderfully relaxed and feeling fine. Five, wide awake.

SHOW CONCERN   *STEP 11*

After the subject is awake, show concern for their well being. *Do not* leave a subject immediately after they are awake. There is a lag period that the subject requires to readjust to their surroundings. While you are waiting for the subject to adjust, *do not* use any negative phrases during your conversation. Use only positive statements, such as, "wasn't that a nice feeling?" It is recommended that you or someone else stay with the subject for at least fifteen minutes after the awakening procedure, in order to cover the lag time mentioned.

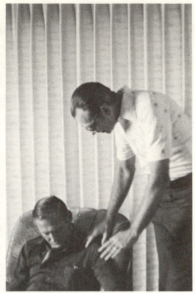

Dr. Kuhns placing a subject
into hypnosis during a law
enforcement teaching session.

Dr. Kuhns being hypnotized by
a sheriff's officer during a law
enforcement session.

Police officer in hypnotic trance for study of Dept. Promotional
Exam or Examination for Sgt.

NOTE: This form can be used twice:
First Time (out of hypnosis)
Second Time (during hypnosis)

SUSPECT DESCRIPTION SHEET

Case No.: _____ Crime: _____

Agency: _____

Hypnotic Subject: _____

Suspect Description:
Height:
Weight:
Sex:
Approximate Age:
Nationality/Race:

Suspect Skin Tone:
Pocked, freckled,
pimples, smooth,
ruddy, fair, rough,
sunburned, windburn

Head Area

Is head: long, short, broad, narrow, large, square, round, inclined forward or backward.
Are ears: big, small, pointed, hairy, other.
Is hair: thick, thin, wavy, curly, parted (how), bald (where), color.

Face Area

Is forehead: broad, narrow, high, low, protruding, bulging.
Are eyebrows: thin, bushy, natural, arched, meeting, slanting (which way).
Are eyes: bloodshot, crossed, squinting, narrow, wide, color.
Are cheeks: fleshy, sunken, drawn, fat, jowls, other.
Are cheekbones: high, pointed, low, unusual shape.
Is nose: thick, thin, long, short, medium, straight, concave, flat, pointed, bent or turned to left/right; nostrils: large, small.

It is suggested that the SDS is to be utilized in Step 1 and Step 9.

Face Area (cont'd)

Is there face hair: moustache, beard, color hair, thick, thin, describe.

Mouth Area

Is mouth area: corners turned down/up, held open/closed, speech pattern, saliva protruding, mouth odor, unusual features.

Are lips: thick, thin, thin-lined, puffy, bulldog syndrome, overhang, is color pale/bright.

Are teeth: False, yellow, white, stained, missing, broken, decayed, filled (color of filling), braces.

Lower Face Area

Is chin: small, large, square, round, curved, pointed, flat, double, protruded, jutted, other (describe).

Is jaw: long, short, wide, other (describe).

Neck to Leg Area

Is neck: long, short, thin, fat (Adam's apple), other.

Is stomach: flat, firm, fat, bulging, flabby, unusual.

Are legs: long, short, skinny, flabby, veined, other.

Hands/Arms Area

Are hands: little, big, long, thin, bony, fat, soft, rough, hairy, unusual, fingers missing, fingers stained (what); nails: long, short, unusual.

Are arms: skinny, fat, bony, soft, rough, scaly, hairy, unusual.

Frame Area

Is build: obese, large, medium, small, thin, skinny, stocky.

Is posture: very erect, unusual stance, stooped, stiff, loose, walk with gait, walk fast/slow/shuffle/limp, use of any walking device.

Cosmetic Devices

Did suspect wear: glasses, hearing aid, facial devices. Do you know if the suspect wore contact lenses; if so, describe.

Unusual Marks

Did suspect have: scars, tattoos, bow-legs, facial injuries, arm injuries, body or leg injuries, other unusual recollections.

Clothing Area

Did suspect wear: pants (color), belt (describe), shoes/boots (color), socks/stockings, shirt/blouse (color) (type), tie, buttons on shirt, (describe) coat/jacket (color), hat (color) (describe).

Jewelry Area

Did suspect wear: watch (describe), ring, necklace, pins, brooches, buckles, other.

Suspect's Vehicle Information

Make:_____ Model:_____ Year:_____

Color:_____ License No. _____ Type of top:_____

Unusual wheels: _____

Unusual exterior items: _____

Any decals or stickers on: windows, bumpers, etc.: _____

_____

Direction of vehicle travel:_____

When last seen: (direction)_____

Number of occupants in vehicle when last seen:

Weapon Information

Type of weapon: ———————————————————

Color of weapon: ——————————————————

Approximate size of weapon: ———————————

How was weapon used: ————————————————

———————————————————————————

Other recollections of weapon(s): ——————————

———————————————————————————

———————————————————————————

HYPNOSIS RETRIEVAL INFORMATION SHEET
— PART THREE —

Hypnosis suggestibility traits: (poor, fair, good, excellent)

Number of Responsive Mental Exercises Administered:_____

Which exercises: Please list: _____

_____

_____

Attitude of subject: (calm, frightened, nervous, other)

_____

Type of induction(s): _____

_____

Changes noted in subject's physical behavior during induction:

_____

_____

Physical movements noted during induction:_____

_____

Deepening techniques administered, please list:

_____

_____

Suggestions given: (list): _____

_____

_____

It is suggested that the HRI sheet part three be completed immediately following the hypnotic session.

Did subject respond to suggestions? (yes) (no)

Challenges administered to subject: (list): _____

_____

_____

Did subject respond to challenges? (yes) (no)

Post-hypnotic suggestions administered to subject: _____

_____

_____

_____

Noted reactions or abreactions to suggestions: _____

_____

_____

(SCALE OF 1 THROUGH 12)

Estimated depth of hypnosis (light 1-4) (medium 5-8)

(deep 9-12):_____

If subject was refractory, Explain:_____

_____

Specific depth scales used: Davis-Husband, LeCron-Bordeaux, Arons, Barber Suggestibility, Standard Hypnotic Suggestibility Scale, Hershman's, other:

_____

Reason for hypnotic session:_____

_____

Information sought: _____

_____

Is there more than one session planned for subject: (yes) (no)

Explain: _____

_____

_____

Any reason for not administering hypnosis at this time?

_____

_____

It is suggested that the HRI sheet part three be completed immediately following the hypnotic session.

Witness in a
homicide investigation,
in hypnotic trance.

This composite drawing was completed from typed hypnosis
statement forms according to Dr. Kuhn's hypnosis format.

An example of composite taken during hypnotic trance when the witness is intentionally giving false information for possible self-serving reasons. The suspect's wife gave this composite to the police artist in an attempt to confuse the entire issue.

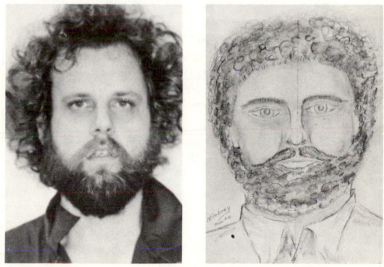

Composite of suspect taken during hypnotic trance and the suspect's actual photo.

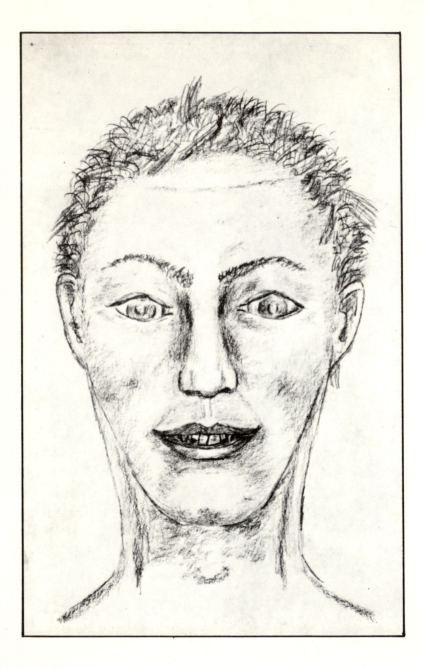

HYPNOTIC DEPTH SCALE #1

Taken from: Davis, L.W. and Husband, R.W., "A Study of Hypnotic Susceptibility in Relation to Personality Traits," in *Journal of Abnormal Psychology*, 26:175-182, 1931.

DAVIS & HUSBAND SCORING SYSTEM FOR HYPNOTIC SUSCEPTIBILITY

DEPTH	SCORE	OBJECTIVE SYMPTOMS
Insusceptible	0	
	1	
	2	Relaxation
Hypnoidal	3	Fluttering of lids
	4	Closing of eyes
	5	Complete physical relaxation
	6	Catalepsy of eyes
	7	Limb catalepsies
Light Trance	10	Rigid catalepsy
(Lethargy)	11	Anesthesia (glove)
	13	Partial amnesia
	15	Posthypnotic anesthesia
Medium Trance	17	Personality changes
(Catalepsy)	18	Simple posthypnotic suggestions
	20	Kinesthetic delusions; complete amnesia
	21	Ability to open eyes without affecting trance

	23	Bizarre posthypnotic suggestions
Deep Trance	25	Complete somnambulism
(Somnambulistic)	26	Positive visual hallucinations; posthypnotic
Trance	27	Positive auditory hallucinations; posthypnotic
	28	Systemized posthypnotic amnesias
	29	Negative auditory hallucinations
	30	Negative visual hallucinations hyperesthesias

HYPNOTIC DEPTH SCALE #2

LE CRON-BORDEAUX SCORING SYSTEM FOR INDICATING DEPTH OF HYPNOSIS

Insusceptible

    0   Subject fails to react in any way.

Hypnoidal

    1   Physical relaxation

    2   Drowsiness apparent

    3   Fluttering of eyelids

    4   Closing of eyes

    5   Mental relaxation; partial lethargy of mind

    6   Heaviness of limbs

Light Trance

    7   Catalepsy of eyes

    8   Partial limb catalepsy

    9   Inhibition of small muscle groups

    10   Slower and deeper breathing

    11   Strong lassitude (a disinclination to move, speak, think or act)

    12   Twitching of mouth or jaw during induction

    13   Rapport between operator and subject

    14   Simple posthypnotic suggestions heeded

    15   Involuntary start or eye twitch on awakening

    16   Personality changes

    17   Feeling of heaviness throughout entire body

    18   Partial feeling of detachment

Medium Trance

19 Recognition of trance (difficult to describe but definitely felt)

20 Complete muscular inhibitions (kinesthetic illusions)

21 Partial amnesia

22 Gloved anesthesia

23 Tactile illusions

24 Gustatory illusions

25 Olfactory illusions

26 Hyperesuity to atmospheric conditions

27 Complete catalepsy of limbs or body

Deep or Somnambulistic Trance

28 Ability to open eyes without affecting trance

29 Fixed stare when eyes are open: pupillary dilation

30 Somnambulism

31 Complete amnesia

32 Systematized posthypnotic amnesias

33 Complete anesthesia

34 Posthypnotic anesthesia

35 Bizarre posthypnotic suggestion heeded

36 Uncontrolled movement of eyeballs — eye coordination lost

37 Sensation of lightness; floating, swinging, or being bloated or swollen; detached feeling

38 Rigidity and lag in muscular movements and reactions

39 Fading and increase in cycles of the sound of operator's voice (like radio station fading in or out)

40	Control of organic body functions (heart beat, blood pressure, digestion)
41	Recall of lost memories (hypermnesia)
42	Age regression
43	Positive visual hallucinations, posthypnotic
44	Negative visual hallucinations, posthypnotic
45	Positive auditory hallucinations, posthypnotic
46	Negative auditory hallucinations, posthypnotic
47	Stimulations of dreams (in trance or in natural sleep)
48	Hyperesthesias
49	Color sensations experienced

Plenary Trance

50	Stuporous condition in which all spontaneous activity is inhibited. Somnambulism can be developed by suggestion to that effect.

HYPNOTIC DEPTH SCALE #3

HERSHMAN'S CRITERIA FOR ADEQUACY OF TRANCE STATES

(Common Order of Learning)

A Light Trance

    1 Relaxation

    2 Eye lid catalepsy

    3 Eye closure

    4 Beginning limb catalepsy

    5 Slowing and deepening of respirations

    6 Immobilization of facial muscles

    7 Beginning catalepsy of limbs

    8 Glove anesthesia

    9 Sensation of "heaviness" in various parts of the body

    10 Ability to perform simple posthypnotic suggestions

B Medium Trance

    11 Partial anesthesia (some subjects)

    12 Definite lag in muscular activity

    13 Ability to accomplish illusions and simple hallucination

    14 Increased "detached" feeling

    15 Marked catalepsy of limbs

    16 Ability to perform more difficult posthypnotic suggestions

C Deep Trance

    17 Ability to maintain trance with eyes open

18 Total anesthesia (in most subjects)

19 Ability to control some organic functions (pulse, blood pressure) etc.

20 Surgical anesthesia

21 Age regression and revivification

22 Positive and negative visual and auditory hallucinations

23 Ability to "dream" meaningful material

24 Ability to perform all or most of the above in posthypnotic state

D Plenary or Stuporous Trance

25 Manifested by marked slowing of all organic responses and almost complete inhibition of spontaneous activity

CHAPTER III

QUOTES: Dr. Bradley Kuhns

*An individual will frequently walk into a wall of truth . . .
But unfortunately, many of them quickly shake their heads
. . . seek and walk in another direction and pretend that
nothing occurred.*

*Everyone tells the truth . . . it's just that many people tell the
truth directly and others tell it indirectly.*

POLYGRAPH AND HYPNOSIS

Many questions are posed as to the methodology of handling
a polygraph examination when dealing with hypnosis, as well
as what approaches to use when the subject is suspected of
using hypnosis to subvert polygraphic testing procedures.
With this in mind, a brief section will describe basic do's and
don'ts regarding polygraph and hypnosis. Emphasis will be
placed on the situation where the polygraph examiner also
acts as hypno-investigator. Please note that this section is not
meant to be an instruction course in the field of polygraph
per se. It is already assumed by this writer that the polygraphers are experienced, trained, polygraph examiners who
already know how to operate the polygraph instrument, but
are interested in acquiring additional knowledge and procedure when confronted with hypnotic techniques.

I should mention that it has come to my attention that there
are some polygraph examiners who have completed only the
30-hour course in investigative hypnosis that was previously
mentioned, returned to their respective agencies and utilized
hypnotic techniques while conducting a polygraph examination. *This is wrong.* Contamination and taint in such a
situation is evident. Further, ignorance of the consequences
of such an act is unnecessary. To this end, I would like to
suggest a format which includes do's and don'ts for the poly-

graph examiner who is also assigned the duties of the hypno-investigator.

Dr. Kuhns is also a member of the American Polygraph Association, California Association of Polygraph Examiners, American Association of Police Polygraphists and past member of the Board of Directors of the California Association of Polygraph Examiners. The type of polygraph examinations conducted by Dr. Kuhns were mostly of a criminal and specific nature. In addition to lectures on the subject of polygraph and hypnosis, he has served on many committees of the various polygraph and hypnosis associations, he has received awards of merit and recognition for his work in both the polygraph and hypnosis fields and has authored articles pertaining to polygraph and hypnosis directed toward continuing education of the respective fields. For the hypno-investigator's reference, a selection of the authored articles include:

a. *Forensic Polygraph as applied to Schizophrenia and Other Behavior Disorders, Phase 1.*

b. *Brain Psychophysiology, c. An overview of Human Behavior.*

c. *Dream Interpretation as applied to Hypnosis.*

d. *A study in the use of Hypnosis to Subvert Polygraphic Findings.*

WHEN THE POLYGRAPHER AND HYPNO-INVESTIGATOR ARE THE SAME PERSON

The ideal situation would be to have two separate individuals administer separate examinations. As referenced earlier, it would behoove the agency to assign two individuals, if for no other reason but to protect the case at issue. When the assigned case investigator also handles the hypnosis session, it invites contamination and taint. The same situation would apply to the polygraph examiner who acts as hypno-investigator or vice-versa. However, it is acknowledged that due to the size and manpower of some departments and agencies, there are investigators that are expected to act in different job classifications and perform dual duties. When this type of situation arises, the investigator should then take every precaution possible to follow a format that will indicate to outside observers that extreme care was exercised in order to protect the subject and the case from taint or contamination.

1. *DO NOT* wear two hats at one time.

2. *DO NOT* incorporate either of the two methods at one time.

3. *DO* approach the matter as two separate and distinct sessions.

4. *DO* secure permission to administer both the hypnosis session and the polygraph examination. (i.e.) From the District Attorney, Police Agency, Court, Opposing Counsel, Subject, and whoever else may be involved, etc.

5. *DO,* at all times, terminate one method of examination completely before proceeding with the second method.

6. *DO NOT* introduce any crime or relevant questions to the subject during the hypnosis session, if the subject is to follow the hypnosis session with a polygraph examination. REMEMBER, HYPNOSIS IS TO RETRIEVE INFORMATION, for recall memory refreshment and memory enhancement. POLYGRAPH USE TO VERIFY INFORMATION. So, use your investigative hypnosis to retrieve the required information. Then, if the information requires clarity or verification proceed with the polygraph examination to verify the extracted information.

Administer your hypnosis session as you would at any other time. Follow your procedure and format, extract the information available, and terminate the hypnosis session. *END OF HYPNOSIS SESSION.* Now, take off the hat of the hypno-investigator and put on the hat of the polygraph examiner. Follow the standard procedure and format that you use and administer your polygraph examination, verify the information, and terminate the polygraph examination. *END OF POLYGRAPH SESSION. Now, you can remove the hat of polygraph examiner.*

GUIDEPOST FOR THE POLYGRAPHER
TO SUSPECT HYPNOSIS

1. When the subject denies *any recollection* or knowledge of the issue at hand, especially when the subject is mentioned in the reports, statements, etc. The possibility would be "Post-Hypnotic Amnesia."

2. When the subject responds with slurred speech, and delayed answers to the examiner's questions during the polygraph pre-test procedures. Naturally, this is assuming that the polygraph examiner has determined the subject is not afflicted with a speech problem. Special note should be taken if the slurred speech and delayed answers occur any time after the instrumental test is begun.

3. When the subject appears to be speaking very softly with the added observation that the subject is experiencing difficulty getting his words out.

4. When the subject sinks down (slumps) into the chair. Either during the pre-test procedure or especially after being attached to the polygraph instrument.

5. Noticeable, dramatic and gross changes in the SRL (Skin Resistance Level) and/or the Pneumograph, and/or the cardio tracing. These changes would be gross and usually exaggerated. Changes very noticeable from the subject's established normal patterns.

6. When there is no evidence of any (SRL) (Skin Resistance Level) response whatsoever, or when there is evidence of

only a very minimal (SRL) response, we can suspect "possible desensitization."

In a case such as this, the subject is usually placed on a biofeedback unit, GSR (Galvanic Skin Resistance) unit and subjected to questions relating to the issue until their physiological reactions are reduced or depleted.

Although there are other signs, both subtle and gross, it is this writer's purpose to alert the polygrapher to the most common ones that may be observed in the event the subject had been hypnotized prior to the polygraph examination.

WHEN THE POLYGRAPHER SUSPECTS THE SUBJECT OF BEING IN A STATE OF HYPNOSIS

1. This writer would suggest that the polygrapher reschedule the polygraph examination at a time (after the subject is dehypnotized).

2. If the polygrapher still has reservations about the subject's outward appearance or the subject's physiological and physical reactions which are thought to be hypnotic countermeasures, further determination by referral of the subject to a medical examination would either confirm or reject the countermeasures of drugs and medications. And, after the medical examination, if the subject was still displaying the outward and physiological signs as before, then it would be recommended that the polygraph examination be rescheduled for a later time.

VARIOUS METHODS THAT HAVE BEEN USED TO SUBVERT POLYGRAPH FINDINGS

1. The hypnotist would instruct the subject to "totally relax on all of the questions," after the subject was attached to the instrument.

2. The hypnotist would instruct the subject to "totally relax on only the relevant or crime issue questions."

90

3. The hypnotist would instruct the subject to have "total amnesia" pertaining to the issue at hand.

SOME EXAMPLES OF HYPNOTIC INSTRUCTION GIVEN TO A SUBJECT PRIOR TO A POLYGRAPH EXAMINATION: FOR THE PURPOSE TO SUBVERT THE POLYGRAPHIC FINDINGS

1. When the examiner states: "The test is about to begin," you will automatically go deep into hypnosis and follow all of the instructions that were given to you here today.

2. You will go deeper and deeper relaxed as the polygraph examiner attaches each instrument component to your body, and (name), when you are completely attached to the instrument, you will be completely and deeply relaxed, in a deep state of hypnosis, and will follow all of the instructions that were suggested to you here today.

3. Amnesia for the entire incident will take place when the polygraph examiner attaches any device or component to your body.

4. You will immediately forget everything about the (issue at hand), when the polygraph examiner attaches any device to your body.

5. You will automatically return to a fully wakened state when the polygraph examiner tells you that the test procedure is over.

SUGGESTED MEASURES TO COUNTER SUBJECT'S HYPNOSIS

1. *DO NOT* administer a closed eye polygraph test when you suspect hypnosis.

2. During pre-test portion of the polygraph examination, inquire about the subject's knowledge of such things as mind control, t.m., autosuggestion, hypnosis, etc.

3. During pre-test procedures the examiner can use phrases

as: "You probably will not be in this room very long, (name), at which time we will *(begin the test)*.

"And, (name), after my explanation of the various psycho-physiological functions and changes that take place in your body, I'm sure that you realize by now that some of those chemical changes that we talked about that occur in your body occur (OPERATOR, SNAP FINGERS) that fast. Yes, the body is such a wonderful machine, and functions with such accuracy, that many of those chemical and physiological changes we discussed happen so rapidly, that they seem to keep a person on their toes (OPERATOR, SNAP FINGERS) and wide awake to things around them.

4. At the conclusion of each polygram, the polygrapher should tell the subject: "That portion of your examination is now complete." It should be noted that subjects have been instructed post-hypnotically to remain in hypnosis until they are told by the examiner that the "exam is completed."

5. During the instrumental testing between each polygram, the subject should be told that the questions will be repeated, and also which order the questions will be in. The polygrapher should also interject the opportunity for the subject to change the wording of the sentence.

The purpose of the above examples is to indicate to the polygraph examiner that the subject may be post-hypnotically programmed for the polygraph test and if the polygraph examiner uses the above recommendations, it can do one of two things. It can either do a great deal to pull the subject out of their hypnosis, or it can confuse the subject's programming, which would have the possibility of carrying the subject to the point of revealing their hypnotic program preconditioning. Remember, when the subject is in your polygraph suite, they are literally on your ground. You as the polygraph examiner can change the polygraph procedure, interject pattern interruption techniques toward the subject, utilize countermeasures that may counteract the subject's countermeasures. It should be worth mention that even though the subject may be hypnotized by a hypnotist, and instructed to follow a program, the hypnotist is limited to what exactly is to be programmed in the subject for specific evasion of the polygraph examination. Remember when it comes down to the bottom line, the polygraph examiner has complete control of the structure, pace and attitude of the examination.

STUDIES OF POLYGRAPH AND HYPNOSIS
FOR THE HYPNO-INVESTIGATOR'S REFERENCE

Studies and Experiments (Polygraph/Hypnosis)

1. KUHNS, BRADLEY, DR.: "A Study in the use of Hypnosis to Subvert Polygraphic Findings" (49 pp) (1978).

2. BRYAN Jr., WILLIAM, DR.: *Florida Experiement,* Miami Police Dept. & Dade County Sheriff's Office (1965).

3. BERRY, ROBERT: "A Study of the Effects of Hypnotically Induced Amnesia upon the Accuracy of the Lie Detector Results (1961).

4. DIEGEL, H.G.: "Prevarication under Hypnosis," Journal of Clinical & Experimental Hypnosis 1 (1953): 32-40.

5. WASHINGTON EXPERIMENT: Examiner was Director of Nat'l Lie Detection Center in Wash., D.C. & Conjoint with Wash. Hypnotic Guild (Mayer/Ziglinski).

6. KRAMER, DONALD T.: "Admissibility of Physiological or Psychologic Truth & Deception Test or Its Results to Support Physicians Testimony." Am. Law Reports (1972) (pp. 1369-85).

7. LONG BEACH EXPERIMENT: GERMANN A.C., DR.: "Hypnosis as Related to the Scientific Detection of Deception by Polygraph Examination, A Pilot Study." Int'l Jour. Clin. Exper. Hypno. 4: (1961) (pp. 309-311).

8. U.S. ARMY MILITARY POLICE SCHOOL, LIE DETECTION COMMITTEE: "Committee Report on the Effect of Hypnotically Induced Amnesia Upon the Accuracy of the Lie Detector Results." Unpublished, Fort Gordon, Ga., Dec. 8 (1960).

9. O'CONNELL, DONALD N./ORNE, MARTIN T.: "An Investigation of Skin Potential Changes During Hypnosis": Public Health Service Grant.

10. ALLEN, KELLY M./GUTMAN, EDWARD G.: "The Polygraph & Hypnotically Induced Repression & Reinforcement." Unpublished manuscript (May 1977) Univ. of Baltimore. NOTE: Poorly written study and experiment.

11. DAVIS, R.C./KANTOR, J.R.: "Skin Resistance During Hypnotic States." Jour. of Gen. Psych. 13, (1935) (pp. 62-81).

12. CORCORAN, JAMES F. / LEWIS / DAVID / GARVER / RICHARD B.: "Biofeedback Conditioned GSR & Hypnotic . . . Suppression of Arousal: A Pilot Study of Their Relation to Deception." Jour. of Forensic Sci 23 (1) (1/78) (pp. 155-162).

CAN PHYSIOLOGICAL FUNCTIONS BE ALTERED BY HYPNOSIS: HERE ARE SOME VIEWS BY SOME OF THE EXPERTS IN THE FIELD

Physiological Experiments (Hypnosis)

1. GORTON: (The Physiology of Hypnosis), Psychiat. Quart., 23: (pp. 317-457) (1949): "States that hypnotically induced emotional changes *can alter* neurophysiological functions and electroencephalographic recordings."

2. FULDE, E.: (Z. Ges., Neurol/Psychiat.) (pp. 159:761) (1937) "Suggested excitement brought about increased respiration."

3. REITER: (Antisocial or Criminal Acts & Hypnosis) (1958) "Suggestions can bring changes in fields of function which are regulated by the involuntary nervous system such as respiration and blood pressure."

4. LEVINE: (Arch. Neurol. Psychiat., (pp. 24:973) (1930) Reports that Galvanic Skin Reflex is subject to alteration under hypnosis. (Electrical Skin Resistance During Hypnosis.)

5. WHITE, M.M.: (Psycho. Bulletin.) (pp. 37:577) (1940) Reported blood pressure & palmar galvanic changes in normal and hypnotic states.

6. LeCRON, L.M.: (Exper. Hypnosis) (1956) Influence of hypnosis on somatic fields.

7. WOLBERG, L.R.: (Medical Hypnosis, Vol. 1) (1948): States that physiological stimulation while the subject is hypnotized produces specific responses which are conditioned by emotional stimulation. But after training, mere

cue words could be used with the subject being in a normal waking state or condition. (NOTATION: Person
could consciously lie and yet control his body so as not
to record a change in any of the recorded factors.)

8. MILLER, N.E.: (1969) Demonstrated autonomic responses such as Alpha Wave, Heart Beat, Blood Pressure, can
be instrumentally conditioned. "A person's blood pressure
can be elevated or lowered by reinforcing him whenever
he emits the appropriate response as increase and decrease
in blood pressure."

9. ELMAN, DAVE: (1964) (Test for Reflex Action in Hypnosis.) Respiration does not decrease, heart action remains
normal, blood pressure remains normal. All functions can
be made to slow down by suggestion BUT, you cannot
get them all to slow down simultaneously as occurs in
natural sleep.

10. KUHNS, BRADLEY, DR.: (Study in the Use of Hypnosis to Subvert Polygraphic Findings) (1978) pp. 44):
Responses nebulous enough to require extensive examination. (Desensitization.)

11. BOYNE, GIL: (1961) Every thought that contains any
emotional content, whether consciously or subconsciously held, causes a physiological reaction.

KUHNS' HYPNOTIC POLYGRAPH
RELAXATION TECHNIQUE

Originated & Developed by
DR. BRADLEY KUHNS

(Name) . . . you will relax . . . (and sleep very soundly tonight) . . . You will feel very relaxed and comfortable in every way for the polygraph examination (test) tomorrow . . . (if applicable, whenever). (Name) . . . during the entire examination (test) procedure, you will feel extremely comfortable . . . serene, . . . perfectly relaxed . . . and content, knowing that the procedure is in . . . skilled, competent, professional hands. The components of the polygraph instrument (machine) will be attached to your body very carefully . . . skillfully . . . and safely . . . and, the polygraph examination (test) will be performed expertly and skillfully. (Name) . . . the test just measures your body responses . . . like any other scientific medical instrument. (Name) . . . nothing on the instrument (machine) will shock you or cause you any physical discomfort whatsoever, in any way. Your complete cooperation will assist the polygraph examiner in concluding the examination (test) in the shortest amount of time possible. The examiner will explain the instrument (machine) to you and the examiner will gladly answer any questions you may have about the examination (test) . . . Remember . . . the examiner is only a seeker of the truth . . . You (name) . . . *will answer any and all questions as you yourself decide and see fit to answer.*

There are no needles or pins stuck in your body in any way. All the instrument (machine) attachments are completely safe and all of the attachments will be attached on the outer part of your body. The instrument (machine) (s) function is just to record your body responses on a piece of paper . . . You, (name) . . . will have the opportunity to discuss and review each and every question that is to be asked on the examination (test) with the examiner . . . even before the test begins . . . In fact, (name) . . . you will know before the instrumental test begins, precisely and exactly what questions are going to be asked on the examination (test). And, (name) . . . when you complete your polygraph test, you will feel very comfortable and very relaxed . . . and, you will feel as though you were sitting in your favorite chair at home. You will feel pleasantly comfortable, extremely full of vim and vigor, full of vitality . . . and, completely revitalized . . . and . . . (name) . . . you will have found the experience to be interesting and fascinating.

THE ABOVE TECHNIQUE CAN BE USED WHEN:

1. Anxiety/emotion are at high levels

2. When the subject's charts are continually inconclusive

NOTE: There is *nothing* mentioned about any specific issue or mention of issue to be polygraphed.

NOTE: There is no taint or contamination by reference to any issue or crime questions.

NOTE: **THE ONLY MENTION OF QUESTIONS** is (specifically generalized). (See the italic portion of technique above.)

NOTE: The only purpose of the technique is to ready a subject for a polygraph examination when they so desire such a test and for some reason or other the subject's anxiety and emotional state tend to be exceptionally high.

NOTE: The word "machine" is used interchangeably with the word "instrument," because it depends solely on how the subjects themselves refer to the apparatus.

CHAPTER IV

HYPNOSIS IN THE COURTROOM

Rather than a large explanation of each and every legal case in which hypnosis was involved, it is the purpose of this writer to cite only the cases which may be of assist to the hypno-investigator, legal counsel, and those concerned. This section is not meant to give an explanation of each case. It is suggested that you research and read the cases as listed so that you can retrieve the specific information you require from each.

1. *People vs. Ebanks:* 117 Cal., 652, (1897)

2. *State vs. Pusch:* N.D., 860, 46 n.w., 2d. 508 (1950)

3. *Cornell vs. Sup. Court, San Diego County:* 52 Cal. 2d. 99, 338 (1959)

4. *People vs. Marsh:* 170 Cal. 2d. 284 (1959)

5. *People vs. Busch:* 56 Cal. 2d. 868 (1961)

6. *People vs. Modesto:* 59 Cal. 2d. 772, 382 P, 2d 33 (1963)

7. *Harding vs. State:* 5 Md. App. 230, 245 A. 2d, 302 Cert. Denied 395, U.S. 949 (1968)

8. *State vs. Jorgenson:* 49 Pac. 2d. 312, Oregon App. (1971)

9. *People vs. Peters:* 4 Crim. 5996, March (1974)

10. *Wyller vs. Fairchild-Hiller Corp.:* 503 F 2d 506 9th. Cir. (1974)

11. *Kline vs. Ford Motor Co.:* 523 F. 2d 1067 (1975)

12. *Jones vs. State:* 542 P. 2d. 1316 (Okla Crime App.) (1975)

13. *People vs. John Quaglino:* 109524 (Sup. Court) Santa Barbara (1976)

It Is Necessary to Lay Foundation for Confidence

In order to give evidence or any information gained through hypnosis credibility in a court of law it must be provided a solid, specific, believable foundation. To do that the person conducting the hypnosis must have a reputation for reliability and be regarded as an expert. This must be clearly established.

He can be a staff member of a police department, but the officer who is in charge of an investigation should not be chosen to hypnotize witnesses because of possible unconscious bias toward a suspect based on "evidence" available at the moment. It is often preferable to have an expert who is independent of the investigation do the hypnotizing and interrogation. (See questions The Court may ask hypno-investigator to determine his qualifications as an expert witness — In Supplemental Data at back of book.)

But whoever is chosen to perform this important task must first acquaint himself thoroughly with the key objectives of the inquiry, and what the witnesses have said about the matter being investigated during prior questioning. This will assure the asking of significant questions and avoiding those not pertinent.

If the questions and answers during the interview under hypnosis are to be recorded by a stenographer or electronic recording device, judicial approval will be required in some states. To obtain evidence for a court of law a recording is essential. Leading questions or any questions suggesting answers other than factual information must always be carefully and skillfully avoided.

A witness should be asked, under hypnosis, if he has been hypnotized previously and if so was any attempt made to induce him to tell anything other than the truth.

Confidence and credibility will be achieved by following the prescribed rules for legal evidence. All evidence obtained by hypnosis should be corroborated.

WHAT IS HYPNOSIS? HOW MANY THEORIES? DEFINE HYPNOSIS

Theories, Definitions (Hypnosis)

1. BERNHEIM: "Hypnotism was a suggestion and there was no marked difference between normal acts carried out under suggestion and acts brought about hypnotically."

2. PAVLOV: Believed that hypnosis was a modified form of sleep.

3. CHARCOT: "Hypnosis is an artificially induced hysteria."

4. FERENCZI: "Hypnotized person has accepted hypnosis by accepting the hypnotist as occupying the place of a parent."

5. SIDIS: "Two parts of the nervous system were dissociated, with primary inhibited and the autonomic open to suggestion."

6. (Another): "Hypnotic trance is nothing but conditioned reflex."

7. HULL & ERICKSON: "Concluded that our present knowledge of human behavior is too little developed to formulate a complete and ultimate theory of hypnosis."

8. HULL: "Chief characteristic of hypnosis is the heightened suggestibility."

9. A. A. MASON: "Hypnosis is a temporary state of modified attention which is characterized by increased suggestibility."

10. (Others): "Hypnosis is a particular state of the nervous system in which the organized inhibition of certain areas permits unaccustomed action. The trance can constitute

one of its characteristics. Suggestibility can be one of its elements, and perhaps also conditioned reflexes."

11. (Others): "Hypnosis is a state of increased receptivity to suggestion characterized by an altered state of consciousness. The degree varies from very light to very deep and usually induces relaxation."

12. BENNETT & VINCENT: "Selective cortical inhibitions occurring in the hypnotic state."

13. B. KUHNS: "Hypnosis appears to be a process where an altered state of consciousness is brought about by various types of specialized and specific stimulation which are markedly repetitive in nature which in turn cause changes in the intellectual and/or motor cortical inhibition which varies in degree resulting in specific changes of stream of consciousness which in chain form may alter volition, spontaneity, mobility and produce an increase of an individual's suggestibility to varying degrees."

14. GIL & BRENMAN: "Hypnosis is a sort of regressive process which can be set off by a reduction in ideational and sensorimotor activity or by creation of an archaic relationship with the hypnotist."

15. MOENSSENS/MOSES/ONBY: "An artificially induced state, resembling sleep, during which the subject is highly suggestible and susceptible to that suggestion, and commands of others."

16. S. J. VAN PELT: "Hypnosis is the name given to that peculiar psychical state in which the mind is particularly susceptible to suggestion."

17. GIL BOYNE: "Hypnosis is a natural state of mind with special identifying characteristics; namely, 1) An extraordinary quality of mental, physical and emotional relaxation, 2) An emotionalized desire to satisfy the suggested behavior, 3) A heightened sensitivity to sensory

and perceptual input, 4) A highly increased responsiveness to suggestion, direction and instruction, 5) Automatic softening of characterological defenses.

Please note that there are many, many other theories and definitions of hypnosis by numerous other authorities. But, it would take many more pages to describe all the theories available.

SOME TERMS DEFINED

From *Webster's Seventh New Collegiate Dictionary*.

"Investigative Hypnosis is solely to assist the individual's re-call, recollection, and refreshment of memory."

RECALL:
    a. To call back (restore, revive).
    b. To bring back to mind.
    c. Remembrance of what has been learned or experienced.

RECOLLECT:
    a. Recover.
    b. To recall to mind.
    c. To remind oneself of something temporarily forgotten.
    d. To call something to mind.

REFRESH:
    a. Revive.
    b. To restore or maintain by renewing supply.
    c. Replenish, arouse, stimulate.

EXPERT WITNESS QUALIFICATIONS

Information on expert witness qualifications described in Case Law and the California Evidence Code:

"A person is qualified to testify as an expert if he has special knowledge, skill, experience, training or education sufficient to qualify him as an expert on the subject to which his testimony relates."

"If the witness exhibits an unusual skill and knowledge, gained from study and experience, not possessed by the man on the street he is competent to give an opinion."

244 CA 2d. 413 (1966)   63 C 2d. 52 (1965)   104 CA 2d. 716 (1951)

EXPERT WITNESS QUESTIONS

1. What is your full name?

2. What is your occupation?

3. Where are you employed?

4. How long have you been engaged in that occupation?

5. Do you use a professional title or hold a rank?

6. What is the highest degree you hold?

7. From what educational institution is your degree?

8. Do you hold any other degrees?

9. Do you have a background in psychology and physiology? If so . . .

10. From what schools or institutions did you acquire that background?

11. Do you hold any license to practice hypnosis?

12. In the course of your education, did you receive any hypnosis training?

13. Where did you receive your hypnosis training?

14. How long were the training courses in hypnosis at the facility?

15. Did you attend any other training courses for the study of hypnosis? If so . . .

16. What was the duration of those courses? Approximately how many clock hours of training time?

17. Did you receive a diploma or certificate certifying the hours or length of time and completion of your hypnosis training?

18. Have you attended any state approved or accredited schools offering specialized training in hypnosis? If so, please explain when and where.

19. Are you a member of any professional organizations dealing with hypnosis? If so, please explain.

20. Do you now, or have you ever held any position with any hypnosis organizations?

21. In the course of your experience in hypnosis application, have you ever received any awards, commendations or titles for your work with hypnosis? If so, what were these awards presented for?

22. Other than the organizations you mentioned earlier, do you hold membership in any others? If so, did you ever hold any position with them?

23. Have you ever given any lectures on the subject of hypnosis? If so, can you recall the topics of the lectures and for whom they were given?

24. Did you receive financial remuneration for these lectures or were they of a volunteer nature?

25. Have you ever held a teaching position at any educational institution or facility wherein you used the subject of hypnosis?

26. Did you ever utilize your hypnosis training for clinical application? Did you ever acquire clinical hypnotherapy training?

27. For whom have you ever conducted hypnosis sessions for the purpose of enhancing memory recall?

28. Approximately how many hypnosis sessions have you conducted since the beginning of your hypnosis training?

29. Out of all of those sessions, did you hypnotize all of the subjects?

30. Can everyone be hypnotized?

31. What is a refractory subject?

32. It would be fair to say then that if approximately _____ % of your subjects were refractory, and may not experience hypnosis to a great extent through an operator on one occasion, that subject may well do so on another occasion or with another hypnotic operator?

33. Have you ever been called upon to testify in court as an expert in human behavior techniques? If so, please explain.

34. Specifically, have you ever been called to testify in court on the techniques of hypnosis?

35. When was hypnosis first used?

36. How widespread is the use of investigative hypnosis in the U.S.?

37. To your knowledge, are there many theories and definitions of hypnosis?

38. What is hypnosis? Can you define it for us here today?

39. What books were used in your hypnosis training?

40. During the course of your hypnosis training, who were the instructors at the facility?

41. Other than the books you told us about, have you read any other books pertaining to hypnosis? If so, please explain.

42. Do you subscribe to or receive any professional journals from organizations dealing with hypnosis?

43. Have you yourself completed any specific studies in the field and techniques of hypnosis?

44. Have you published or written any articles on the use of hypnosis?

45. Can anyone lie under hypnosis?

46. When did the American Medical Association first recognize hypnosis?

47. When did the British Medical Association first recognize hypnosis?

48. Are there any depth scales that are used in the practice of hypnosis?

49. Which depth scales are recognized by the profession as a whole?

50. What type of induction did you use when inducing hypnosis on Mr._____?

51. Did you acquire a release of any kind from Mr._____ _____prior to any hypnotic session?

52. Did you explain the hypnotic procedure and/or the techniques to Mr. _____ prior to any hypnotic session?

53. Did you use a deepening technique in Mr._____ session? If so, please explain.

54. What suggestions did you administer to Mr._____ _____in the hypnotic session?

55. What post-hypnotic suggestions did you administer to Mr._____in the hypnotic session?

56. Did you utilize any test procedure that would be indicative of Mr._____suggestibility to hypnosis? If so, which ones?

57. Would you say that as a practical matter, the integrity of hypnosis operators using "investigative hypnosis techniques" is high?

58. Would you say that by talking to a hypnosis operator and looking into his experience using hypnosis, one could make a fair determination as to whether or not he or she is competent?

59. Out of all the hypnotic sessions that you have conducted,

how many in your opinion were considered to supply new information?

60. How did you verify the depth of hypnosis Mr._____ _____ experienced?

61. Can the operator be fooled by the subject who is faking hypnosis?

62. Did you use a specific hypnosis technique when hypnotizing Mr._____?

63. Are you aware of any scientific studies that demonstrate the validity and reliability of this technique?

64. On what types of cases have you used "investigative hypnosis" since your initial training?

65. What methods are there to deceive the hypnotic operator into believing that what the subject states is being derived while in a hypnotic state?

66. Can you administer hypnosis to anyone that doesn't want to undergo the procedure?

HYPNOSIS AND STATE LAWS

While the author was serving as chairman of a school approval committee, the following material was researched and compiled from information furnished by the Attorney General's Office of each state. It was believed to be accurate to date during the time the research was being compiled.

By **Dr. Bradley Kuhns**
F.A.I.H., F.A.C.M.H.

Alabama: From the Attorney General's Office: "Alabama has no law concerning . . . hypnosis."

Alaska: No information available

Arkansas: No laws prohibiting hypnosis.

Arizona: No laws prohibiting hypnosis.

California: "The practice of hypnotism is not prohibited by state law unless such practice constitutes an unauthorized practice of medicine or psychology."

Colorado: "While in general there are no regulations of hypnotists, depending on the particular actions taken hypnosis or hypnotherapy could fall within the definitions of medicine, psychology or social work."

Connecticut: "There is nothing in the Connecticut General Statues that deals with this specific concern." *(Quote from a letter from the Attorney General, Law Librarian)*

Delaware: No laws prohibiting hypnosis.

District of Columbia: No information available.

Florida: "Hypnosis may be practiced by a licensed professional or by a 'qualified person' (deemed to be so by the referring practitioner) who is competent to employ hypnotic techniques for therapeutic purposes, under supervision, direction or prescription.

Statement: It shall be unlawful for any person to engage in the practice of hypnosis for therapeutic purposes unless such person is a practitioner of one of the healing arts, as herein defined, or acts under the supervision, direction, prescriptions, and responsibility of such a person." (Chapter 456)

Georgia: "A review of the Georgia laws reveals that there is no provision pertaining to hypnosis or hypnotherapy." *(Quote from the Attorney General)*

Hawaii: No laws prohibiting hypnosis. However: A person "practices 'Psychology' who performs any professional service which consists of, requires, and is limited to the application of psychological principles and procedures for the purpose of understanding, predicting, or influencing behavior of an individuals in order to assist in their attainment of maximum personal growth; optimal work, family, school and interpersonal relationships; and healthy personal adjustment. The application of psychological principles and procedures includes . . . hypnosis."

Idaho: No laws prohibiting hypnosis.

Illinois: No laws prohibiting hypnosis.

Indiana: No laws prohibiting hypnosis, however, from the Office of the Attorney General we received the following:
"Depending upon the extent of your claims for and on behalf of hypnosis, it is possible they should also inquire of the Indiana Medical Licensing Board which is located at the same address as the Psychology Board." But, (Definition):

"The law essentially states that no one may call himself a psychologist, psychometrist, or any variant thereof or render services which are described as psychological or any variant thereof if the person so doing is not a licensed psychologist. The act specifically exempts teachers of institutions of higher learning recognized by the Board but even those individuals cannot style themselves psychologists or their services psychological without being licensed psychologists."

Iowa: From the Office of the Attorney General: "I am not aware of any statutes in Iowa relating to the teaching or practice of hypnosis. However, if an individual uses hypnosis to treat a human ailment, that individual may be in violation of the various practices acts in Title VIII of the Iowa Code."

Kansas: No specific statutes prohibiting hypnosis; except that Section 21-4007 "Hypnotic Exhibition" is a Class C misdemeanor. This means that no one can "give for entertainment any instruction, demonstration or performance in which hypnosis is used or attempted." Interpreted to mean that no hypnosis is allowed.

Kentucky: "We have found no specific laws in Kentucky applicable to the use and/or teaching of hypnosis and hypnotherapy."

Louisiana: The teaching of hypnosis comes under the jurisdiction of our Proprietary School Commission. No laws prohibiting the use of hypnosis.

Maine: No laws prohibiting hypnosis. From the Office of the Attorney General:

"Maine law does not make specific reference to the practice of hypnotherapy in this state. Regulation of the practice would likely fall under the Jurisdiction of the Board of Registration in Medicine and/or the Psychologists Examining Board."

Maryland: "There are no statutes concerning the use and/or teaching of hypnosis and hypnotherapy."

Massachusetts: No laws prohibiting hypnosis, however, from the Office of the Attorney General: "Section two to six, and section eight shall not be held to discriminate against any particular school or system of medicine . . . persons practicing hypnotism, magnetic healing, mind cure, Christian Science or cosmopathic method of healing, if they do not violate any provision of the preceding section."

Michigan: No laws prohibiting hypnosis, however, from the Office of the Attorney General: "This state does not specifically license the practice of hypnosis as a distinct activity."

Minnesota: "Minn. Stat. SS 147.10 (1976) is the only Minnesota statute that specifically addresses hypnosis. Basically, that statute provides that no one other than physicians or psychologists licensed in Minnesota may use hypnosis 'for the treatment of or relief of any wound, fracture, or bodily injury, infirmity, or disease.' "

Mississippi: No laws prohibiting hypnosis.

Missouri: No laws prohibiting hypnosis.

Montana: From the Attorney General's Office: "I am aware of no laws in this state which specifically regulate the use of hypnosis or hypnotherapy."

Nebraska: From the Attorney General's Office: "You will not violate any state laws by holding a two-day informational meeting in Omaha."

Has only prohibition of "exhibiting person in trance." "We cannot determine whether they (other laws regarding the practice of medicine and/or psychology) affect the use and/or teaching of hypnosis here."

Nevada: From the Attorney General's Office: "Nevada has no state laws on the subject of hypnosis and hypnotherapy."

New Hampshire: From the Attorney General's Office: "It has been determined by the Board of Registration in Medicine that hypnosis and hypnotherapy are part of the practice of medicine and can be performed only by someone who is licensed to practice medicine in this state."

New Jersey: No laws prohibiting hypnosis.

New Mexico: (Our letter was referred to the Board of Educational Finance/Commission of Post-Secondary Education) Their comment: "No laws prohibiting hypnosis."

New York: From the Attorney General's Office; "Unless the members of your staff are licensed physicians, they may not lawfully use hypnosis nor teach the use of hypnosis in this State."

North Carolina: No laws prohibiting hypnosis.

North Dakota: No laws prohibiting hypnosis.

Ohio: "Ohio Revised Code — Section 4732.01 (C) includes hypnosis within the definition of "psychological procedures."

Oklahoma: No laws prohibiting hypnosis.

Ontario, Canada:
Section 2:
Subject to Section 3, no person shall hypnotize or attempt to hypnotize another person. 1960-61,c. 38, s.2.

Section 3:
Section 2 does not apply to:
(a) any legally qualified medical practitioner;
(b) any dentist registered under the Dentistry Act;
(c) any psychologist registered under the Psychologists Registration Act.

Oregon: Oregon Revised Statues 167.870 regards hypnosis as prohibited. References are only made to "exhibiting person in trance," "exertion of the will power or suggestion of another person over such subject, or consents to or aids or abets such exhibition."

Pennsylvania: "Although no licensing statutes apply directly by their terms to hypnosis, presently it is conceivable that a number of statutes could be so applied.

Rhode Island: No laws prohibiting hypnosis.

South Carolina: "We find no statute in the South Carolina Code of LAWS, or any published opinion of the Attorney General, which would apply to the question . . . "

South Dakota: (Similar law to Oregon's) Statue Numbers are: 22-20-1 to 22-20-3.

Tennessee: No laws prohibiting hypnosis. The Attorney General supplied the following quote: "Due to manning and budgetary constraints, we regret that this office cannot provide legal advice or assistance to private entities."

Texas: No laws prohibiting hypnosis.

Utah: No laws prohibiting hypnosis.

Vermont: No laws prohibiting hypnosis.

Virginia: Section 18.2-315 is the only section of the Virginia Code dealing with hypnotism. (The use of hypnosis) "But this section shall not apply to hypnotism or mesmerism performed at the request of the patient by a licensed physician, licensed clinical psychologist, or dentist, or at the request of a licensed physician in the practice of his profession."

Washington: "A search of Washington statutory and case law indicates that there is no Washington Law dealing specifically with hypnosis or hypnotherapy. No laws prohibiting hypnosis.

West Virginia: "The West Virginia statute is silent upon the subject of the practice or use of hypnosis, and the absence of any statute controlling same has not been interpreted by the West Virginia Medical Licensing Board as vesting in it the authority to authorize the practice or use of hypnosis."

Wisconsin: Wisconsin does not have any statutes specifically relating to the teaching or use of hypnosis and hypnotherapy. "However, it is clear that an individual cannot engage in the practice of same for the purpose of attempting to cure or treat

the physically or mentally ill without being under the supervision or direction of a
licensed physician or psychologist or psychiatrist.''

Wyoming: No laws prohibiting hypnosis.

EDITOR'S NOTE: Since new legal decisions about hypnosis are being handed down currently in many states, I urge the reader to use this information as a guide and to request current information from the State Attorney General's Office and other appropriate agencies.

STATE OF OREGON   Oregon Legislation, June 23, 1977
A-ENGR. HB 3125

SECTION 1. If either prosecution or defense in any criminal proceeding in the State of Oregon intends to offer the testimony of any
person, including the defendant, who has been subjected to hypnosis,
mesmerism or any other form of the exertion of will power or the
power of suggestion which is intended to or results in a state of trance,
sleep or partial unconsciousness relating to the subject matter of the
proposed testimony, performed by any person, it shall be a condition
of the use of such testimony that the entire procedure be recorded
either on videotape or on any mechanical recording device, and that
such unabriged videotape or mechanical recording be made available to
the other party or parties in accordance with ORS 135.805 to 139.990.

SECTION 2. (1) No person employed or engaged in any capacity
by or on behalf of any state or local law enforcement agency shall use
upon another person any form of hypnotism, mesmerism or any other
form of the exertion of will power or the power of suggestion which is
intended to or results in a state of trance, sleep or entire or partial unconsciousness without first explaining to the intended subject that:

(a) He is free to refuse to be subject to the processes delineated in
this section;

(b) There is a risk of psychological side-effects resulting from the
process;

(c) If he agrees to be subject to such processes, it is possible that
the process will reveal emotions or information of which he is not consciously aware and which he may wish to keep private; and

(d) He may request that the process be conducted by a licensed
medical doctor or a licensed psychologist, at no cost to himself.

(2) In the event that the prospective subject refuses to consent,
none of the processes delineated in Section 2 (1) shall be used upon
that person.

SECTION 3. No evidence secured in violation of sections 1 or 2 of
this Act shall be admissible in any criminal proceeding in this state.

114

CONFIDENTIAL INVESTIGATIVE
HYPNOSIS REPORT

RPD Case #0000 K 79

RE: Doe, John
       WMA, Age 18 years
       Witness

SUBJ: Homicide

On December 2, 1979 at approximately 9:30 AM, an Investigative Hypnosis Session was administered to the above named subject. The Hypnosis Session was administered at the request of Detectives Teglia and Penegor of the Reno Police Department, Detective Division. The Investigative Hypnosis Session was conducted by Dr. Bradley Kuhns at the Reno Police Department Facilities. The purpose of the Investigative Hypnosis Session was to determine if additional information could be retrieved to assist the Reno Police Department in their ongoing investigation pertaining to the issue at hand. Prior to any hypnotic inductions, a pre-induction session was conducted in which the procedures of the Investigative Hypnosis Session were explained, including the areas that were to be looked into while this subject was in the state of hypnosis. The subject also had an opportunity to ask and have answered any and all questions pertaining to the entire procedure that was to be undertaken. In addition, prior to the Investigative Hypnosis Session a Consent and Release Waiver was obtained from the subject.

During the pre-induction session, the subject made the following relevant statements in regards to the issue at hand pertaining to the crime of homicide. Doe's information was directed to the specific areas of possible identification of motor vehicles at the scene of the homicide. In reference to

NOTE: Names have been changed for report data and individuals' protection.

the vehicles this subject states his recollection as follows: Vehicle #1 was described as a small, red sports car with a black top. Vehicle #2 was described as a blue van, dirty and dusty. He went on to state that the vehicles were observed by him as he drove into the parking lot at the location where the crime occurred on November 19, 1979. This subject had no further information to offer as to the identification of the two vehicles observed at the scene. Since the subject made no further relevant statements in regards to the motor vehicles that were said to be at the scene, an Investigative Hypnosis procedure was then undertaken with the subject's permission. Recognized inductions and standard techniques were utilized, and the following information was elicited from the subject while under hypnosis.

In reference to Vehicle #1, subject described the following: a) a red sports car, b) very red and shiny with a black top, c) subject recognized an emblem on the hood of the red sports car, d) the emblem was described as a round, chrome emblem. In reference to Vehicle #2, the subject described the following: a) a Ford van, 1973 or 1974, blue in color and dirty — "I know it's a Ford because I saw it," b) the taillights of the van were round, c) license plate of the van was described from left to right as WS 1 6 or 9 4 2. The background color of the license plate was described as dark blue. The letters and the numbers of the license plate were described as white in color. The subject also indicated there was no license plate holder on the vehicle, and the license plate was in the center of the rear bumper of the vehicle. During the Investigative Hypnosis Session on further close-up inspection the subject described a red sticker located in the upper right hand corner of the rear plate, and the red sticker was described as having the numbers 1-80 imprinted on the red sticker. The numbers 1-80 were said to be black in color. In addition, the subject described the wheels of the vehicle on the passenger side as having regular tires, and further described the rear wheel on the passenger side as having a hub cap, white in color. Doe also described the passenger side of the vehicle as having a large dent to the rear but below the lower half of the vehicle. He also indicated there was no hub cap on the front wheel of the passenger side of the vehicle. Subject also described the vehicle as being "dusty dirty" rather than "muddy dirty." This subject made no further relevant statements pertaining to the issue at hand, and since no further information was elicited at this time from this subject while he was in the hypnotic state, the subject was then awakened with recognized and standard wake up procedures, and a post-test session was then conducted.

During the post-test session, the subject indicated that he was surprised at the recollection and recall that was available from the Investigative Hypnosis Session. He also made the statement that he would be available for further interviews regarding this matter should the Department feel the need to call on him for assist. This subject was also left with the post-hypnotic suggestion that if recollection or recall of further information to the issue at hand should occur within the next few days no matter how insignificant, he was instructed to contact the investigating officers with this new information. At the completion of the post-test session the subject was excused, and the Investigative Hypnosis Session was then concluded.

END OF REPORT

Dr. Bradley Kuhns
Reno Police Department
Behavior Science/Polygraph Section

NOTE: Dr. Bradley Kuhns is presently employed with the Los Angeles Police Department and assigned to the Scientific Investigation Division. He is also Director of the Institute for Professional Research and Evaluation.

NOTE: Names have been changed for report data and individuals' protection.

HYPNOSIS STATEMENT
Including An Actual Composite Description

RE: DOE, Jane   RPD Case #0000 L 79

Knowing now, knowing now Jane, that we are going to put that face, going to transpose it on a piece of paper, so that it can be developed into a picture, and all your problems may be resolved with your assistance and cooperation. Mr. Bennett is just going to ask you some questions, you will be glad and willing to answer them very clearly and plainly. He is an expert in his field, you will be able to talk to him or any one of us in this room, up until the time that I tell you to go back into a deep comfortable sleep. Do you understand? That's right just relax now. Now, I want you to concentrate on the violent one. You have him in your mind, your subconscious already notified me of that. The more you describe him to Mr. Bennett the more clear and vivid, the more clear and vivid that picture will become, the more clear and vivid it becomes, the more detail you will remember, the more detail you remember Jane, the more accurate it will be. And after you describe everything to Mr. Bennett, I will have you open your eyes and then you are going to actually correct anything that may seem off to you, anything that may seem off, after he shows you a drawing, you will be able to correct, very easily because that picture will be frozen in your mind. We will just transpose it from your mind to that paper. After he shows you a complete artist's sketch, if there are any changes, you will feel very comfortable and calm in telling him what to change to make it more perfect. Ok, Bill Bennett is going to talk to you Jane, you will be able to answer him very easily. Go ahead, Bill.

Q. *Jane, when you first saw this person, the violent one, how far away was his face from your face?*

NOTE: *Names have been changed for report data and individuals' protection.*

118

A. We were right close up, for about two minutes.

Q. *Ok, could you smell any odor about him?*

A. No.

Q. *Ok, when he looked at you did he say anything?*

A. Exactly when?

Q. *From the very first meeting you had with this person.*

A. He told us both to walk down the alley.

Q. *Ok, at that time were you looking at his face?*

A. No, he made us dig through our purses first.

Q. *I didn't hear you.*

A. I said, he made us dig through our purses first.

Q. *But, when you were looking at his face, did he say any-thing to you, when you were looking at his face? When he told you to dig through your purse?*

A. Yea.

Q. *Now, when you first saw the man's face, if I were to ask you to describe the man's face, could you describe the man's face to me?*

A. Yes.

Q. *Ok, was his face thin, or was it fat and round?*

A. It was very thin.

Q. *Is it thin like a sick person with the cheeks high and lines or hollowness underneath the cheeks?*

A. No.

Q. *What was his color like? Was the color in his face good color or was it sallow? Or was — go ahead.*

A. He was very dark.

Q. *Very dark?*

A. Not black.

Q. *But, very dark.*

A. Yea.

Q. *Ok, now if you will, we will look at the man's face and we will start right in the middle of his head where his hair line comes down. Do you remember what his hair line looked like across the top of his face? Did he have curly hair, did it come over his forehead?*

A. No, it was parted in the middle and came over both sides.

Q. *Parted in the middle and came over both sides.*

A. Yes.

Q. *Ok, as you come down the forehead, right straight down, you get to the nose, how much distance between the forehead, the top of the forehead and the nose was the eyebrow line? Where you come down the eyebrow.*

A. Like this?

Q. *Yes, right down like this. Was it long or was it short? In other words did he have a broad forehead, narrow or small forehead?*

A. Broad.

Q. *Broad, ok. Now we will stop there, and we will go back to the top of the forehead and we will make a circle starting from your left. You put your left hand straight up and touch his forehead and as you come down in a circle you come down to his ear. Did he have side burns?*

A. No.

Q. *Was he clean shaven?*

A. No.

Q. *Ok, you say he was not clean shaven, what was wrong with his face?*

A. He had a little bit of a moustache, not very much, just like he hadn't shaved in a couple of days.

Q. *Ok, now where on his, if you were looking at his, if you were looking right at him, we're over on the left side of his face, and I'll touch your left arm to tell you that is the side of the face I'm talking about. I'm coming down from the center of his forehead, and his hair is parted in the middle, I'm coming down to almost to the ear. Now does the hair continue on down past the ear, like a side burn?*

A. No, it was short.

Q. *It was short?*

A. Yea.

Q. *Ok, now did you, can you tell me what his left ear looks like? Does it stick out from his face? Or is it close to his forehead, I mean to the sides of his face, can you see the earlobes — the bottoms of his ears?*

A. It was very small, very small ears.

Q. *Very small ears. Ok, now going down the sides of his cheeks, you said that there were two or three days stubble on his face?*

A. Yea, but it was, but it was not that hard.

Q. *It was not that hard? It was kind of soft?*

A. Yea.

Q. *Ok, how old was this fellow?*

A. I'd say about, somewhere around 20.

Q. *He was around 20, ok, now you come down to his cheek bones, where his cheek bones on the left — did it stick out? Could you see the muscles in the sides of his cheeks? And I'll touch your cheek where I mean. Right here, did you notice anything on his cheek, did his line come down or did it protrude? In other words was he full cheeked, full chin, did he have a strong jaw?*

A. It was, I don't know how to describe it, it was out like this (subject using her hand to describe).

Q. *Ok, now we will come out to the chin, did he have any markings on his chin?*

A. No.

Q. *Did he have a line in the center of his chin, approximately here? Or was his chin round?*

A. No, it was pretty much round.

Q. *Pretty much round ok. Go back up the other side now, we will come up the jaw line, it's about the same as the other side. Alright?*

A. Yea.

Q. *Ok, we go up to the other ear, did you notice anything about the other ear? We will continue up the other side of the head now — go up to the forehead — the center —*

121

right in the middle of the forehead, come down and look at the nose again. Can you describe his nose? Was it long, was it small, was it broad and flat, or was it like a Roman nose, like a boxer. Can you describe his nose?

A. It was skinny and kind of long, he did not have a bump right here, it was kind of like a point but not really.

Q. *There was nothing wrong, he had not been injured in any way.*

A. No.

Q. *Was it like a girl's nose, or a man's nose, was there heaviness to it or was it thin and light?*

A. It was thin and light.

Q. *Now his eyes, go back to his eyes, anything unusual about his eyes? When I say unusual were they large, small, anything unusual, long eyelashes, did he have long eyelashes?*

A. No. But he had thick eyebrows.

Q. *Thick eyebrows. Did his eyebrows come together in the center?*

A. No. They came to about right here, I guess.

Q. *Were they thick on the outside, or towards the center?*

A. Towards the center.

Q. *Did you notice any bagging or scars underneath his eyes?*

A. There were bags, no scars or anything.

Q. *Bags, under his eyes — were they real noticeable or just slight?*

A. They were just slight.

Q. *Now we go down to his nose, and his face, do you feel by looking at him was everything in proportion, was he, did he have big eyes for his nose, or did he have a big nose for his eyes, can you tell me that?*

A. Just about normal.

Q. *We will go down to his mouth now. Was there anything unusual about his mouth?*

A. No.

Q. *Ok, how about the space between the tip of his nose to the top of his upper lip?*

A. No.

Q. *Ok, we're going down, I'm looking at his teeth. When he spoke to you the first time, to look through your purse, did you notice anything unusual about his teeth?*

A. No.

Q. *Did you see his teeth?*

A. I don't remember that.

Q. *Don't remember his teeth, you think about that now. Normally when a person talks to you the first time, especially when they are giving you orders for some reason or other you seem to look towards their mouth anticipating the next word. Take yourself back to that point and listen for his words. Listen to what he said to you. Can you hear him saying something to you? Look at his mouth now Jane, is there anything unusual about his mouth? Take your time now.*

A. They are kind of jagged.

Q. *They are kind of jagged, the teeth?*

A. Ya.

Q. *Are they dirty or clean?*

A. They have rotten spots on them.

Q. *They have rotten spots on them? Now how about the hair on the moustache area? You said he had an unshaven look of two or three days of growth on his face. On this described person which is Latin or Spanish I'll touch your face. Did he have more hair in the outer area, or was it straight across? Do you understand what I'm talking about?*

A. Uh-huh.

Q. *Think back, look back to when you first saw him and look particularly between his nose and upper lip.*

A. I'd say that it was mostly on the outer area.

Q. *On the outer area.*

A. But it was not that thick.

Q. *Was not thick — like a fuzz, or a soft hair.*

A. Yea.

Q. *Now you say that the hair was fairly short, was it a — was there anything unusual about the length of it?*

A. No.

Q. *You have no sideburns, the hair was not long in the back? Just an average hair cut. Yet you think it was parted in the middle and was on both sides.*

A. Yes.

Q. *But you saw no scars, no tattoos, no pachuco marks on the cheeks, nothing like that? But you noticed — was there anything about his breath? You noticed nothing about his breath?*

A. No.

Q. *Ok, I'm talking to you now, and I'll talk to you later and you will remember what I said now and I'll ask you other questions, but I want you to picture in your mind or in your head, exactly the first image you had of this person. And I'm doing this because most people don't realize it, but the first image you have of a face is usually your best recollection. Now will you concentrate and think of that face, and the next time that I talk to you I'll bring this up to you. Can you do that?*

A. Uh-huh.

Q. *Ok.*

(Kuhns speaks) Now Jane, take a deep breath for me. Ok, before we turn you over to Bill later on — I want you to concentrate on the violent person once again. We did not get what type of clothes he was wearing. So let's back off for a second and see him full length. Jane, let's start with like cutting down a tree or building a skyscraper. Let's start with his feet, 'cause you have already described his head. Right? Let's start with his feet.

Q. *What's the guy wearing on his feet — the bottom.*

A. Tennis shoes.

Q. *Is there a special color?*
A. I think they are black with white tips on the ends.
Q. *Ok, that's fine. Now as you are looking at him full length — what type of pants does he have on?*
A. Levis — like . . .
Q. *Any color?*
A. Blue.
Q. *Ok, you're doing fine, Jane, just relax and you're doing fine — no problem. Now, take a look around his waist — do you see any belts? Any buckles?*
A. No.
Q. *Ok, just look above his waist — what strikes you above his waist — his shoulders — what is he wearing?*
A. A white tee-shirt, like a wind jacket — with a zipper.
Q. *A wind jacket with a zipper — that's great, Jane. Is there anything on the zipper, like some people have strings or leather tongs or something tied to them?*
A. Don't see anything.
Q. *Does it have pockets?*
A. Yes.
Q. *Where at?*
A. Right here. [Subject used hand to describe.]
Q. *On the side?*
A. Yea.
Q. *Square ones, or the ones you put your hands in diagonal.*
A. Diagonal.
Q. *Ok, what color is this wind breaker?*
A. It was a dark color.
Q. *Ok, it's ok — ok so he has a white tee-shirt, dark colored windbreaker. Is he wearing anything around his neck — like a piece of jewelry? Or a choker chain? Anything?*
A. No.
(Detective Dan Tapia asks)
Q. *Ok, Jane, on the jacket was it padded or a thin windbreaker like mine.*
A. I think it was padded — yes.

(Kuhns asks)

Q. *Padded. One of the heavy ones like they wear in the mountains?*

A. No not heavy like that — just has a little lining like — tuffs.

Q. *Oh, like tuffs. Ok. Was he wearing anything else besides the Levis? White tee-shirt — windbreaker? What hand did he have the glove on?*

A. The left hand.

Q. *What color was the glove, Jane?*

A. Black.

Q. *That's great, I'm proud of you. Just relax, you are doing fine. You really are.*

(Detective Tapia asks)

Q. *Was the glove leather — cloth, or what?*

A. Leather.

Q. *Did it look like a ski glove or a tight fitting glove?*

A. Tight fitting leather glove.

(Kuhns asks)

Q. *Did you see any rings, watch or anythign on his hands that rings a bell with you?*

A. No.

Q. *No watches or rings? Were they carrying anything else besides having a gun in their hands?*

A. No.

Q. *Ok. How are you doing?*

(Bennett states) He is going to start three different sketches in his mind — then when he comes in she is going to work with one and they will go from there with it, so go ahead and take your time — he is going to start the three drafts.

(Kuhns states) We've got on this violent one that we did not have before now — tennis shoes, blue Levis, white tee-shirt — and a jacket — windbreaker — dark colored with tuffs.

(Detective Tapia states)

Q. *Jane, did this fellow have flared leg or straight leg Levis?*

A. It was flared leg.

Q. *Flared leg. Was he wearing anything on his head — I forgot to ask you this.*

A. No.

Q. *Any details or anything marked on his jacket? Some things . . . . Look at the right and the left sides of the jacket, Jane, just the pockets, not the chest. Look right at the chest.*

A. There were not any pockets on the chest.

Q. *Ok, look up by the chest where pockets usually are, what I'm saying — any decals that you can see?*

A. Just plain.

Q. *If you ever think of the color before you leave, it will automatically pop into that mind of yours and you will be able to tell us what color it was. Ok?*

(Detective Tapia asks)

Q. *Do you remember anything on the violent subject's face — scars — pock marks or pimples — little zits or whatever?*

A. No.

Q. *I think you said before, Jane, that this one was the subject that talked with a little bit of an accent — is that correct?*

A. Yes.

Q. *Do you remember any particular word that he said that made you think that he had an accent?*

A. No.

Q. *He sounded like a Mexican — Spanish accent? Right? How bad was it?*

A. It was not that bad at all. It was kind of mild.

(Kuhns asks)

Q. *Jane, would you like another Coke — a cigarette?*

A. Yes.

Q. *See there — that's easy to do — watch what is going to happen — you will be surprised and amazed. Here is what is going to happen — In a very short time — maybe about one minute — I am going to have you open your eyes, but you will not open your eyes until I tell you to.*

END OF STATEMENT . . . Subject brought out of trance with I.S.S. applied for instant re-hypnosis.

STATEMENT OF JANE DOE CONTINUES: Subject returned to trance.

(Kuhns speaks)

Q. *Ok, Jane, let's pick up where you said you saw these Mexicans. Is that what you said they were?*

A. This is when we were past Sierra Canes — that I seen the one Mexican and the one Black, over to the right. Then we just kept walking. These guys were coming towards us — we figured that they would pass by. They had their hands in their pockets. One — both of them had one glove on each hand. There was like only one pair of gloves —

Q. *Are you trying to see another one — that's alright — one pair of gloves?*

A. Yes.

Q. *Ok, just look at them — take your time — they are going to stay — it's in your mind — we will see them there —it's alright. They can't go anyplace now we have them locked in — in that mind — don't we? Just take your time looking at them — they can't run away — they can't do a thing. As long as you bring them back to that frame. You could stand back and look at them for hours on end and they can't even move.*

A. I can't really see them I'm just describing them.

Q. *Where are you at on 4th Street?*

A. It's about 2 blocks from Circus Circus.

Q. *Ok, who is with you?*

A. Stacy.

Q. *Can you tell me what Stacy is wearing?*

A. She has on a white coat.

Q. *And?*

A. What's she wearing? Pair of blue jeans and on the back it has on the pockets — it has like —rainbow stripes. A red coat.

Q. *Are you walking towards Circus Circus? When are you first aware of these two males — these two boys — Jane?*

A. When we are walking down the street and they got inside — got —

Q. *Ok, is that better on you? [Dr. Kuhns dims room lights.]*

A. Yes.

Q. *That's what I thought. Now that your eyes are more comfortable — When is the first time that you were aware of these two?*

A. When we were walking along — you know when you are walking down the street and everything — you don't figure that the person walking towards you — is going to pull a gun.

Q. *So they are walking towards you — you didn't think they were going to pull a gun, is that it?*

A. Yes.

Q. *Ok, it's alright — you are doing fine now. Just relax. Watch how much more clear and vivid it's going to become. In fact you are going to feel more relaxed aren't you. You will relax deeper — Ok, walking closer to you now. What are you thinking? You are talking to Stacy — you are thinking something. What?*

A. We were mad — because um,

Q. *Why are you mad?*

A. Well our boyfriends were playing poker — and we were sitting in the kitchen where they were sitting. My boyfriend goes — why don't you and Stacy go sit in the living room so we can get down to some serious poker playing. Then got mad.

Q. *So they are losing their money?*

A. I got mad 'cause he didn't want us in there watching. So me and Stacy left. We just started walking.

Q. *When you first saw these two guys what were they doing?*

A. They had their hands in their pockets.

Q. *Were they walking towards you — or on the other side of the street?*

A. Same side of the street.

Q. *Same side. Ok, as they got closer what did you say? You and Stacy were talking about them. What did you say about them?*

A. I don't know, we were just talking.

Q. *Ok, as I snap my fingers, you are automatically going to remember what happened as soon as they approached you. I am going to snap my fingers and you are going to see the men approach you — and talking to you. What is the first thing you recall that they said? I wonder which one talked first? (KUHNS SNAPS FINGERS.)*

A. The violent one — the one that — as they were coming towards us the one on the right hand side.

Q. *The violent one — what did he say?*

A. He wanted us to give him all of our money.

Q. *He ordered you to give him all of your money?*

A. Yes.

Q. *He was on the righthand side, is that it?*

A. On the right hand side.

Q. *Walking towards you.*

A. Yes.

Q. *Ok, when he ordered you to give him the money, Jane, what else did he do?*

A. Wait a minute . . . first he said both of you two walk down this alley.

Q. *Ok.*

A. It was over to our right. By the railroad tracks.

Q. *Both of you walk down this alley — and it was over to your right?*

A. Yes.

Q. *Ok, visualize — look to your right — and see yourself going down the alley — now what is happening? You are going down the alley.*

A. I've kinda fallen behind, and whining and he says stop whining and he hit me. He pushed me up forward.

Q. *Now, which one was this? The calm one or the violent one?*

A. The calm one. Also, right after the calm one pulled the gun — he put his mask on right afterwards.

Q. *He put his mask on?*

A. Yea.

Q. *Ok, what kind of mask did he put on, Jane?*

A. It was a ski mask with eyeholes — and —

Q. *He put his ski mask on — is that before he took you down the alley?*

A. It was while we were going down the alley.

Q. *Ok, that was the calm one.*

A. Yea.

Q. *Who pushed you? Was it the calm one or the violent one?*

A. The calm one.

Q. *Ok, now you are in the alley — tell me what is happening.*

A. They stop by a shed — and as we were going — as we were walking down to the shed — they made us take — take everything out of our purse. We didn't have anything except for Cheap Trick tickets. We gave them those, and then when we got down to the shed — the violent one got really mad because all we had was those tickets which only added up to $18.00 — he kept saying 18 lousy dollars — you poor broads.

Q. *What do you remember?*

A. He just keeps kicking the shed. Saying that we belong in the slums — we are just as poor as they are.

Q. *Did he look poor?*

A. Yea.

Q. *What is your girlfriend doing while this is happening?*

A. She just keeps trying to empty out her purse, saying we

don't have anything. She had three cents in her purse. She tried to hand it to him and he threw it out of her hand.

Q. *Just take a minute and take a deep breath. Relax, you are doing fine. Now what I am going to do — is I am going to transfer some of my permission over to my friend here — Dan — you met him earlier — he is going to ask you a couple of questions. You will answer him just like you answer me. Nothing is going to bother you — 'cause I am here with you, ok?*

(Detective Tapia asks)

Q. *Jane, can you tell me the color the ski mask was on the violent subject?*

A. It was the calm person that had the mask on.

Q. *Ok, do you remember what color that mask was?*

A. It was a dark color — dark blue I think.

(Dr. Kuhns asks)

Q. *Can you tell me what he was wearing other than the mask?*

A. I think he was wearing jeans —

Q. *Blue jeans?*

A. Yes.

Q. *Blue jeans and a blue mask. Was he wearing a coat?*

A. It was like a — not a — like . . . really smooth jackets — I don't know what they are like, like suede maybe.

Q. *Like suede?*

A. No, not really . . . smoother.

Q. *Smooth jacket.*

A. Like a rain coat. A windbreaker.

Q. *Do you remember how long it was?*

A. It was about down to here I guess. [Subject indicates by pointing.]

Q. *What about his shoes, Jane, do you remember? What kind of shoes was he wearing? Watch what happens — we are going to back it just a little bit where you can see his entire body. Just scan — like you are looking up and down his entire body at his clothing. Shoes, boots, san-*

dals, whatever you are aware of.

A. I think they were tennis shoes.

Q. *Tennis shoes, ok, now before he put on his mask could you tell me what nationality he was. Do you know what I am saying when I say nationality. What nationality do you think he was?*

A. Mexican.

Q. *Now, before he put on his mask — can you tell me anything about — his facial features?*

A. He might have had a little bit of a moustache. Like he had not shaved in a couple of days.

Q. *That was the calm one, huh?*

A. Yea.

Q. *Go ahead, you were going to tell me something?*

A. They were both really skinny, and their hair was kind of short — it was dark —

Q. *That's ok Jane, that won't bother you. Did he have any scars or pimples, or funny teeth or anything that you can remember? As your impression — females always look at guys — you know that — now, what struck you about him, if anything, besides being skinny? What was it?*

(Detective Tapia asks)

Q. *Was he wearing something in his ears — anything like that? Did he speak with an accent? Spanish accent? Or did he just look like he was Mexican?*

A. The calm one didn't speak like that — like he had an accent — but the other one did.

Q. *The violent one did? Yes. What about his hair? . . . The calm one?*

A. It was like — about like Tapia's hair.

(Kuhns asks)

Q. *Ok, like Tapia's hair. Ok you have given me the jacket, shoes, and pants. Can you tell me by chance what he was wearing underneath his jacket? Could you see that?*

A. They both look alot alike — except the violent one is taller.

Q. *Was he wearing a hat that you know of?*

133

A. Which one?

Q. *The calm one. We will work on the violent one later 'cause he is the nasty one. We will work on the calm one now.*

A. The calm one put — he had — his mask was not on top of his head — it was in his pocket. And then after we started walking down the alley — he put it on.

Q. *Ok, was he dark or fair complected?*

A. He was pretty well — a little bit darker than me.

Q. *A little bit darker than you. How old do you think he was — the calm one.*

A. I'd say between 19 and 22.

Q. *Had you ever seen him before.*

A. No.

Q. *Would you know it if you did?*

A. Not really.

Q. *How about jewelry — that's on the calm one — see any watches? Rings? I.D. bracelets? Anything that struck your eye, because once again you are a girl — and boy — you have to be given credit for that intuition you have.*

A. Nothin'.

Q. *Was the calm one the one with the gun?*

A. They both had guns.

Q. *They both had guns? Was the calm one wearing any gloves?*

A. There was one — ok, the calm one had a glove on his right hand and the other one had a gun in his left hand. They both — the calm one had a glove on the right hand — the other one had a glove on the left hand.

Q. *Did the calm one hold the gun in the gloved hand or the other hand?*

A. The gloved hand.

(Kuhns asks)

Q. *Do you remember anything about the gun?*

A. It was just a small one and had a barrel — (POINTS TO CYLINDER AREA OF GUN).

Q. *Cylinder, is that what you are trying to say?*

A. Yea.

Q. *What color was it?*

A. Black.

Q. *What about the grips — did you see what kind of grips the gun had? That's the handle.*

A. Yea.

Q. *It's ok — just take your time — we are going to talk to this man — relax — you are going to relax with each breath.*

Q. *I asked her about the grips on the calm subject's gun . . .*

A. They both had the same kind of gun.

(Tapia asks)

Q. *Did they — ok, about how long was the barrel — can you estimate, Jane? Was it a real long barrel — or kind of a short one? You can use your fingers if you want to.*

A. It was short.

Q. *Do you know anything about guns?*

A. No.

Q. *I just wonder if these guys look the same — both carrying guns. I am going to ask you questions about the violent one. Did he have his mask on all the time?*

A. He didn't have his mask on.

(Kuhns)

Q. *Ok, just relax — get into any position that you want. You are comfortable and calm. You are doing ok. Which one, Jane, actually took your purse — and was going through you purse?*

A. (Inaudible) The violent one was going through Stacy's purse. He was throwing everything all over.

Q. *Ok, was he throwing everything all over as he was walking along the track?*

A. Yes.

All set, Bill? Yes, I'm going to take her out of here and go to another room. I would like her totally conscious, because we are going to sit and build something together. I want her now to concentrate. I want to talk to her when she is conscious — the questions that I ask are — just to refresh — to start her thinking. Brief me for an instant. I have to talk to her. [DR. KUHNS BRIEFS COMPOSITE ARTIST, THEN INSTRUCTS HYPNOTIC SUBJECT.]

Q. *Just relax, take a deep breath. You are doing fine. Just relax. You are doing fine. In a moment I am going to introduce you to Mr. Bill Bennett — he is a police artist. You will be able to listen to him and understand each and every word he says — anything he asks you will be able to answer very clearly and plainly for him. Now, basically what we are going to do is focus on that violent person. I want you to visualize in your mind's eye now that violent person — the one without the ski mask — now what I'm going to do is touch this finger over here. When you can see that man — the violent one — the first time you see him close up — I want that finger to start to raise for me. You will relax deeper as that happens — as soon as you see that man in your mind's eye — close up — that finger will begin to raise automatically, without any help on your part — it will automatically start to raise. That is the violent one, Jane, the violent one.*

END OF REPORT. The subject then refined and corrected the police artist's composite to reflect the accuracy as she recalled it to her memory.

Composite armed robbery suspect given under hypnosis by
Jane, who was later murdered.

NOTES OF DR. KUHNS
APRIL 18, 1980
PERTAINING TO THE INDUCTION OF SUZIE

Since the child was 3½ years old it was assumed that her complete attention and concentration were required. The induction included attention-getting techniques to have the child follow along with mocking patterns. The complete attention counterpoint was the fact that the examiner was to direct specific attention to the exact spots where the child's attention was to be. This in turn convinced the child that the games were serious and that the examiner had a great interest in her, (i.e.):

Not right there, right here, give me your finger, right there. And, look me in the eye. Not that eye, this eye right here where I'm pointing.

The direction to specific areas convinced the child that the examiner was interested, and later would work for waking and re-induction methods.

NOTE: Names have been changed for report data and individuals' protection.

INVESTIGATIVE HYPNOSIS REPORT
SUPPLEMENTAL

RPD Case #000D 80

RE: Suzie
      WFJ Aprx. 3½ years
      Witness

SUBJ: Missing Person
       Possible Homicide

Now Suzie, we're going to play a game and it's a game you're going to like. Now hold your finger just like this. Now when I count to three, touch your nose. That's fine. Now when I count to three you're going to touch the top of your head. One, two, three. Not there, right here, give me your finger, right there. Now, Suzie, put your hands down and look into my eye. Not that eye, this eye right where I'm pointing. Right here, that's right. Now, I'm going to touch you very lightly right there. When I do you're going to close your eyes. You're going to feel very, very sleepy. When I press your hand and take my hand away, your hand is going to feel very light and it's going to go up into the air. And now Suzie you're going to go to sleep. You're becoming more sleepy than ever, just like when you take a nap in the afternoon. Now you're asleep and you're going more and more and more into a dreamy, dreamy sleep.

Now Suzie, from those games that we played earlier, from those games we played earlier you're now going to dream. And as you dream about them you're going to be able to talk to me very clearly and hear everything I say. Suzie, now that you're sound asleep and dreaming like we talked about earlier,

---

NOTE: Names have been changed for report data and individuals' protection.

139

you're going to be able to tell me all about the trip you took
with Daddy — the trip that you mentioned earlier. Are you
ready? Go ahead.

Q. *Now, Suzie, what are you aware of? Suzie, we're getting*
   ready to go on a trip. How are you going on the trip?
A. In car.
Q. *Who's with you?*
A. Poppy.
Q. *Who's Poppy?*
A. Poppy, Daddy.
Q. *Suzie, as we talked about it earlier you'll be able to sleep*
   soundly in that chair and you'll be able to describe that
   trip that you and Poppy took. Do you understand?
A. Uh-huh.
Q. *Now, Suzie, how long do you think it took to take that*
   trip?
A. A long time.
Q. *Can you tell me with your fingers how long?*
A. This many [child holds up four fingers].
Q. *How many is that, Suzie, that you're holding there?*
A. Four. Poppy said four or five hours.
Q. *Suzie, did Poppy tell you why you're going on this trip?*
A. Uh-huh.
Q. *Why?*
A. To see Auntie.
Q. *Where does your Auntie live?*
A. I don't know. A long way.
Q. *Suzie, now I want you to see your trip very clearly and*
   very plainly. Are you doing that?
A. Uh-huh.
Q. *Did you stop anyplace after you left your house on your*
   way to your Auntie's?
A. Uh-huh.
Q. *Can you tell me where?*
A. In the desert.
Q. *Suzie, can you tell me why you stopped?*

A. Yeah.

Q. *Why, Suzie?*

A. I smelled poo-poo in the car.

Q. *Poo-poo?*

A. Uh-huh. [Child began to fidget and move.]

Q. *Suzie, I am now going to touch you on the top of your head. And, remember it will be the same spot where you touched yourself before. It has to be that exact same spot. When I do you will want to open your eyes. Then after we talk awhile, I'll let you close your eyes and go back to sleep like this again and we will continue to talk. Is that o.k. with you?*

A. Uh-huh.

Q. *Suzie, only when I touch you on that exact spot will you open your eyes. Now let's see if that will be the exact right spot. [Dr. touches child on the head in spot where agreed earlier. Child opens her eyes.] Was that the right spot?*

A. Yeah, see my eyes?

Q. *Suzie, would you like a drink of water?*

A. O.k.

FIVE MINUTE BREAK . . . Talk about nursery school.

Q. *Alright, Suzie, remember when we were playing those games before and I placed a spot on the back of your hand?*

A. This one. [Child points to a small spot made earlier with a felt tip pen.]

Q. *That's it, that's the one. Now Suzie, that spot that's on the back of your hand, right there, that spot that we placed there when we were playing games. Look hard at that spot, 'cause it's slowly going to come up and it's going to come closer and closer to your forehead and your face. The hand is going to start to raise. Just keep watching the spot, Suzie. And, the harder you try to get away from that spot the faster and faster it's going to*

141

move towards your face, Suzie. And, when you feel your hand touch your face you're going to close your eyes and your head will become very heavy and tired like it was before. And you're going to go to sleep even much faster than you did before. That sleep is going to be even much deeper than those naps you've taken in the afternoons. This sleep is going to be where you're going to be able to hear me, your friend, talking to you very clearly and plainly. That's fine Suzie, now that you're asleep very deep you're going to be able to remember very, very easily now all about that poo-poo that you told me about before when you were dreaming. Now, you're going to be able to tell me when you first smelled that poo-poo and what your daddy "Poppy" said about it. That poo-poo smell. Where did the poo-poo come from?

A. The back of the car.

Q. *Did you ask your daddy what the poo-poo was?*

A. Yeah.

Q. *What did Poppy tell you?*

A. Poppy said it was a dead animal.

Q. *Suzie, did Poppy tell you what kind of a dead animal?*

A. Uh-uh. No.

Q. *Besides stopping in the desert, Suzie, did you stop anywhere else?*

A. Uh-huh. Yeah.

Q. *Can you tell me where? Now, Suzie, Just watch that trip you're taking very carefully, very clearly, o.k.? And, it will become more clear to you and you will be able to describe everything to me that you really remember.*

A. Okay.

Q. *Now, where else did you stop, Suzie?*

A. We went camping.

Q. *You went camping?*

A. Uh-huh, and swimming.

Q. *Do you know where?*

A. In the woods.

Q. Did you like to go camping?

A. Uh-huh, with Poppy.

Q. Can you tell me where you're camping?

A. Uh-uh.

Q. Is it close to Auntie's house?

A. Uh-huh. A long way from my house.

Q. You did very well, Suzie, you did very, very well. Now, in a little while, you're going to open your eyes again, but not until I touch you very lightly right here on that spot. And, Suzie, when you open your eyes and when you leave here you're going to be very, very happy. In fact, all day long while you're in this police station talking with those women and policemen out there you're going to be very happy and you're going to like everybody and everybody will like you while you're here in this building. And, before you go home you're going to ask for a drink of water and you're also going to ask for some more candy. You're going to be very happy and surprised that those police officers out there in that other room will give you more candy and water. Now Suzie, with a big smile, and right now open your eyes. There, isn't that fun? Did you have fun here today?

A. Uh-huh. Yeah.

END OF REPORT

Dr. Bradley Kuhns
Reno Police Department
Behavior Science/Polygraph Section

INVESTIGATIVE HYPNOSIS REPORT

RPD Case #000 D 80

RE: Suzie
       WFJ Aprx. 3½ years
       Witness

SUBJ: Missing Person
        Possible Homicide

On April 18, 1980 at approximately 3:30 p.m. an investigative hypnosis session was administered to the above named subject. This session was administered at the request of Sgt. Pete Henry and Detective Gary Eubanks, Detective Division, Reno Police Department. The investigative session was conducted by Dr. Bradley Kuhns and the hypnosis session was administered at the Reno Police Department facilities. The purpose of this investigative hypnosis session was to determine if additional information could be retrieved from the subject Suzie to assist the Reno Police Department in their ongoing investigation pertaining to the issue at hand, that being a missing person possible homicide. Prior to any hypnotic induction a pre-induction session was conducted to determine if the subject would be suitable for an investigative hypnosis session due to the subject's age of approximately 3½ years. A pretest interview was conducted specifically to determine if the child could comprehend time, places, time frame and surroundings. The pretest interview session satisfied this examiner that the young child would be suitable for an investigative hypnosis session. Information sought from witness Suzie was any recollections, recall, information regarding her father, the suspect in the case, any recollections,

NOTE: Names have been changed for report data and individuals' protection.

recall or information of her mother, known as Ellen, missing person in the case at issue. Recognized inductions and standard techniques were utilized; it should be noted that due to the subject's young age of approximately 3½ years, a very light state of hypnosis was induced. The young child proved to be a good hypnotic subject, in relation to her age, intellect, personality and projection. During the pretest interview session, the young child indicated that she does not live with her mother, however she did state she liked her mother and her mother traveled a lot. She said her mother is always going to the airport. At the time of this interview she said she did not know where her mother was. Subject went on to say she did like her father, whom she refers to as "Poppy." During the present interview session the subject was very cooperative and showed this examiner that she could write her name, explaining that she did go to a school named Small World. She did appear to be very eager to display talents of spelling and singing.

INFORMATION ELICITED FROM THE SUBJECT DURING HYPNOSIS SESSION

A. The child recalls a trip with her father, known as "Poppy." The child indicated the trip took approximately 4 to 5 hours.

B. The child indicated the trip was for the purpose of going to see her aunt. The child could not recall or recollect where her aunt lived.

C. During the automobile trip the child stated she and her father stopped one time in the desert. The child also indicated that during the automobile trip her father also stopped to go camping and swimming.

D. The child also indicated that during the automobile trip she did smell an odor in the car which she described as "poo poo." She said that her father told her it was a "dead animal" that caused the smell.

No further relevant information was elicited from this young subject so she was then awakened with recognized and standard wake up procedures at which time she was left with a post-hypnotic suggestion that she return to the front office of the facility, request a piece of candy from one of the investigators, continue to play games and be happy until she was returned to her residence where she would have dinner. The young subject was then excused and the investigative hypnosis session was concluded.

Dr. Bradley Kuhns
Reno Police Department
Behavior Science/Polygraph Section

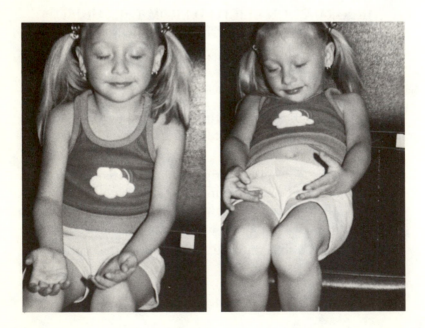

INVESTIGATIVE HYPNOSIS REPORT
SUPPLEMENTAL

Case #G00082 WCSO

July 23, 1980
RE: Daiton, Pat
     Victim
     WFA-30

SUBJ: Armed Robbery

Now Pat, please fix your gaze on that little object that you see there. Continue to sit perfectly still and keep looking; as I count each number you are going to relax and become very, very comfortable and soon your eyes will close and you will just drift off into a very deep, comfortable sleep and that sleep will be very restful and relaxed feeling and you will be aware of everything I say and everything you do. Now on one just keep staring at that spot and the odds right now are that you are going to feel a little silly and you are smiling. That is perfectly all right, in fact it is going to relax you even more. Just go on looking at that spot and listening to the sound of my voice as I count each number — 1 — 2 — 3 — now you are listening to my voice, my voice is very prominent — now we are going to reverse the numbers from 10 to 1. Listen to the sound — and listen to the sound as I count and that smiling will just help you relax more — just smile whenever you feel like it. Whenever you hear my voice it is going to be very calming to you — now all the time keep looking at that spot and eventually you are going to relax very comfortably and you are going to quit smiling. Your eyes may get tired and want to close — if they do it is alright to let them close. After you have no inclination to smile, you can let your eyes close.

NOTE: Names have been changed for report data and individuals' protection.

And about 7 when I get to 7 your eyes may feel like they are becoming very heavy and three or four counts from there, that spot may become very bright and some other things in the room may become very, very shadowy and dark and finally just before your eyes close and don't want to stay open any more everything will become basically dark black in the peripheral area of your vision. It will appear as though you are looking down a long, long tube or tunnel with a small, bright light at the end and you are going to feel very comfortable and relaxed. In fact as I count each number — 10 — 9 — 8 — there is — 7 — my voice will become softer, possibly it may sound just a little smoother to you now as your breathing changes and after your eyes close my voice may sound very close to your ear, but then sometimes it may sound as though it has receded and comes from clear across the room and as I count each number smaller — 6 — and — 5 — and — 4 — your body may feel as though it's becoming so heavy and sinking so deep into that chair that you can hardly move — now that your eyes are closed your shoulders and arms are relaxing — 4 — you are aware of your breathing now and very comfortable and very slow — 3 — in fact notice that tingling on your lips right now — 2 — and you are comfortably relaxed — just letting go every muscle and every fibre in your body — 1 — and — 0 — now you are aware of the sound of my voice, your eyes are closed and you are coming more relaxed and letting go and sinking deeper into the chair — feeling good — feeling calm — feeling serene. Now that you are very relaxed sitting there you can feel so comfortable now you may feel a small glowing feeling there — watch that feeling as it spreads — just let it spread up and down your entire body, in fact your chest is now relaxing and that belly is just loose and limp and relaxed and it is spreading and spreading through the back. Let go completely now Pat — you are doing fine — that pelvis and the thighs — in fact your muscles will totally let go. Just like little rubber bands representing each of those muscles and muscle fibres — one is released and the whole thing totally relaxes — so totally let go. Now that the relaxation has spread completely up and down and throughout your body I know now and you know now that you feel completely relaxed and you are going deeper and into a very comfortable and relaxed state — every sound of my voice will just help you to relax deeper now, Pat. Now notice that your mind is much quieter — your mind is much quieter as you move toward that restful peaceful sleep state. Nothing matters now, nothing at all — everything is so calm and peaceful — any sound outside that room is just going to go by you like water off a duck's back. Now you can keep your eyes closed and maintain your relaxation that you can speak very easily, very plainly, just as though you are talking in your sleep and you can tell me all about your experiences that we are going to discuss about that specific day of July 20, 1980. And now, Pat, I am going to show you how your body functions can work and how the mind can work to such a degree that your body can do many fantastic things and you are still aware of what is happening — now I want you to concentrate and while you are concentrating — I'm going to concentrate on your right hand and as I touch you very lightly in this special spot on your right hand you are going to feel a lightness develop in that hand — in fact your hand may very well start feeling like it is very light — just like an airy balloon and in a very short time that right hand movement is going to develop and you are going to feel that hand rise in the air all by itself without any effort on your part — there it goes it's moving now, in fact it is going to float higher and higher just like a feather in a breeze — just like it is made out of styrofoam, it's lifting, rising and going up, and it will move faster and faster and higher and higher and float right up straight in the air as though you are reaching for the ceiling — just as though you are reaching for the ceiling. That's it — now — watch what happens when I touch you very lightly in that specific spot on that hand again. Make a fist — that's right — make a fist of the right hand as though you are trying to punch an object hanging

149

from the ceiling. Now I will touch your arm in another specific spot and the next time that I touch your arm it is going to become as stiff as a bar of steel. Just like a steel rod — so stiff you couldn't bend that arm no matter how hard you try — no matter how hard you try — you can't bend that arm. That's good, that's fine, you are doing great. Now the next time I touch your right arm in that special spot it is going to return to normal and it is going to relax very comfortably and very easily into your lap and as it floats and lowers very comfortably and very easily and safely into your lap you are going to relax much deeper into that state of relaxation. Now as I promised you earlier, Pat, I want you to realize that you will never be hypnotized while driving a car or by stage hypnotists — you will always be in a safe and secure place and no one can ever hypnotize you or put you in a state of relaxation such as this unless they have the training that you would expect. Each time that you are in this state of hypnosis you are going to go into it much easier, much more quickly and much deeper each and every time — remember each and every time we work together you will enter this state of hypnosis much more quickly, much more deeply and much more soundly each and every time. In fact it will be unnecessary to go through long processes from now on — that special key that I worked with you earlier is going to work very easily for you from now on. When I utilize our private special key in this building, no matter what you are saying — no matter when it is you will immediately stop what ever you are doing and close your eyes and enter a state of sleep even deeper and deeper than the one you are in right now. In fact your eyes will close and you will instantly drop to the deepest level you have reached in the past and then we can always start from that level. We can always start from that deeper level.

[COMPOSITE COMPLETED.]

Now that you have described the suspect that took all that

money from your cashiers' cage on July 20, 1980 — you can be very proud of yourself — that picture will remain in your mind and should you ever see that person again no matter how briefly — you will automatically recognize him and after you recognize that person you will have the desire to call any law enforcement agency or specifically the investigating officers you have been talking to in regards to this case and you will relay the information to those officers. You are also going to find now that you have described this person to me in the state of hypnosis and relived the entire incident as it happened, that you are going to find yourself living with the situation and coping with it much better. You are going to find yourself not being so tense when people walk up to your cashier's cage from now on. You are going to find yourself more relaxed, more comfortable — projecting your personality and just placing this incident in the back of your mind as though it happened a long, long time ago. But remember, should you be questioned in regards to this matter by any law enforcement agencies or authorities you will be able to reach into your memory banks and recall all the information as accurately and as vividly as you did here this evening. In fact, Pat, all the information you recalled this evening will remain very vivid in the corner of your memory for future recollection. You are going to find unless you need that material that you now recall — for information to the authorities — it will remain in that one section of your mind very comfortably. It will remain in your subconscious just as all the other things out of your life remain in your subconscious without worrying you or bothering you or disturbing you in any way whatsoever. But should you have to recall any of this specific information that you have related to us here this evening you will be able to describe and recollect all the information in the same vivid, accurate detail as you did this evening, and you will find that you will be able to do that without adding or deleting. And, now that you know you can feel comfortable in your own mind living with what happened and coping with what happened — you are going to look forward to going back to your job in the cashier's cage and doing the best job that you ever thought possible. You will project your personality and have a feeling of well being toward all the customers that you confront on a daily basis. Now in a moment I am going to wake you, but to prove to you beyond all doubt that you have been successful here today you are going to be able to see very clearly now the artist's sketch that you have given us in this state of hypnosis — the police artist will show you this sketch after you are totally wide awake and you can be happy in your own mind that you cooperated with the authorities in this matter. Now as I promised you as you entered this state of hypnosis, I'm going to prove to you beyond all doubts that you have been successful today — I'm going to give you a post-hypnotic suggestion and that suggestion will be carried out immediately upon your awakening, and then you know in your own mind that I am a man of my word and that you have proved successful and you can be assured that all of the suggestions that I have given you will be carried out because I say that they will be carried out, and you can be assured that any suggestions that were meant for your wellbeing and benefit that were accepted will likewise prove very successful to you. On the count of 5 you will be totally wide awake and you are going to be normal in every way shape and form — spiritually, physically, psychologically and emotionally. You are going to be normal in every respect but one — you are going to find it very difficult to open your eyes and the harder you try the more difficult it will become. They are going to remain closed until I touch you on the forehead, and as I touch you on the forehead, I'm going to say the words "Pat Daiton" — so your eyes will stay closed until I touch you on the forehead and say the words "Pat Daiton" — and then they will open very wide and very clear and you are going to be totally wide awake. And after you awaken you are going to feel that you are very comfortable, feeling very enthusiastic and very alert and in fact very excited and very happy remembering every word that I have said — you are going to feel very refreshed, extremely alert and clear headed and feeling normal from head to toe in every way — strong and refreshed in your mind, your body, and your spirit, and in every other way that you can think possible. Now Pat, 1, 2, 3, 4, 5 — that's right but those eyes won't open, will they — Pat Daiton — now . . . 5. Wide awake, totally wide awake — that's it, Pat.

END OF REPORT

Dr. Bradley Kuhns
Reno Police Department
Behavior Science/Polygraph Division

NOTES PERTAINING TO THE CASE:

The composite taken from subject while under hypnosis was shown in and around the area of the robbery the following day. A suspect that matched the composite was arrested and taken into custody.

From all information received thus far, the suspect underwent two polygraph tests in regards to the issue at hand and was found to be untruthful on both exams.

The actual amount of time the victim was exposed to the suspect during the crime was approximately one minute.

INVESTIGATIVE HYPNOSIS REPORT

WCSO Case #0000082

July 23, 1980
RE: Daiton, Pat
     WFA-30

SUBJ: Armed Robbery

On July 23, 1980 at approximately 6:30 p.m. an investigative hypnosis session was administered to the above named subject. The hypnosis session was administered at the request of Officers Mike Barbarigos and Bob Beeghley — Washoe County Sheriff's Office — Crystal Bay, Nevada. The investigative hypnosis session was administered at the Reno Police Department facilities. The purpose of the investigative hypnosis session was to determine if the victim Pat Daiton could formulate a composite sketch of the alleged suspect of the armed robbery. The alleged armed robbery was said to have occurred on July 20, 1980 at approximately 1:05 p.m. The estimated loss during the alleged robbery was approximately $24,500.00. Prior to any hypnotic inductions a pre-induction session was conducted in which the procedures of the investigative hypnosis were explained, including all areas that were to be looked into while the subject was in the state of hypnosis. At the same time the subject had an opportunity to ask and have answered any and all questions pertaining to the entire procedure that was to be undertaken. Present during the procedures of the hypnotic session were:

A. Dr. Bradley Kuhns — Reno Police Department
B. Police Artist — Reno Police Department
C. Bob Beeghley — Washoe County Sheriff's Office
D. Hypnotic subject Pat Daiton

NOTE: Names have been changed for report data and individuals' protection.

During the preinduction session of the investigative hypnosis session the subject made the following relevant statements in regards to the issue at hand. Pat Daiton indicated that she only saw the alleged suspect committing the armed robbery for a period of approximately one minute. She could not formulate any specific recognizable description to assist the officers in the identification. Dr. Kuhns utilized recognized inductions and standard techniques were also utilized and a complete composite artist's sketch of the alleged suspect was elicited from the subject while under hypnosis. The composite was a complete front facial view from the head and shoulders of the alleged suspect. Once Miss Daiton completed her description of the alleged suspect and a composite drawing was as complete and as accurate as possible pertaining to Miss Daiton's recollection she was then awakened with recognized and standard wake up procedures at which time she was left with the post-hypnotic suggestion that should she recall anything pertaining to the issue at hand no matter how insignificant it may seem to her she was to contact the investigating officers handling the case and relay all the information to them. After Miss Daiton was brought out of the hypnotic state a brief post test session was conducted during which time the subject was allowed to become fully awake and cognizant of her surroundings. She was then returned to the care of Sheriff's Officers to be transported and returned to her residence. The investigative hypnosis session was then concluded.

END OF REPORT

Dr. Bradley Kuhns
Reno Police Department
Behavior Science/Polygraph Section

INVESTIGATIVE HYPNOSIS SESSION

July 2, 1980
RE: Hall, Jeff
SUBJ: Attempted Murder/Robbery

Now Jeff, I want you to silently count from 100 backwards to zero. And as you're silently counting, you're going to drift into a very comfortable relaxed state of hypnosis and should you miscount anyplace along the way or even hesitate or forget your count, you'll automatically go deeper and that's because I said you will. And when you do miscount or hesitate or skip a number I'm going to touch your forehead and when I do you'll just relax even deeper into the state. Now start counting silently and mentally back from 100. That's right, nod if you're at 50, I'm going to touch you lightly on the forehead again and you're going to drift still deeper into a very relaxed state. Now, drift deeper, there you go. While you're in this safe, comfortable, relaxed hypnotic state you're drifting deeper and deeper with each and every breath you take. With each and every sound of my voice you're drifting even deeper and you're going very deep into a— and Jeff, when I count to three you're going to open your eyes feeling very, very sleepy but very anxious to go right back into that very comfortable calm relaxed feeling that you're in now, even deeper than before. In fact, you're going to go much deeper the second time when I count to three. Now, Jeff, as I count one, two, three you're feeling even sleepier and more anxious to go right back into that deep, deep, relaxed, comfortable state that you were in before, but even much deeper than before. And now Jeff, as I count to three you can close your eyes and very quickly and easily enter a state of sleep, even deeper than you've been before. One, two, three. That's it, even more comfortable and deeper than you were before. Now, Jeff, let everything else recede into the background, let everything else recede into the background. Just listen to the sound of my voice. Think of my voice as a cool, cleansing breeze blowing through your mind. Blowing away all the cobwebs. In fact, Jeff, there will be nothing you will want to withhold or hide from me as we discuss what happened on that specific date and time.

Now, Jeff, your entire mind is a great mass of tapes and these tapes are divided and separated by each and every year. Now, can you see these tapes? When you do, this finger I'm touching right now will automatically begin to move upward. That's right, those tapes are divided and separated by each and every year. Now, select the tape that has 1980 on it. The year 1980, Jeff, when you have that tape that says 1980 this finger again will begin to rise. Now, Jeff, take that tape from 1980 and put it on the machine. It's one of those modern video cassette machines, we can speed up the tape, we can slow down the tape, we can even zoom in and freeze any frame at any time. We can freeze the frame, we can freeze the action, we can even turn up the sound. So, Jeff, now that the tape of 1980 is in the machine, as I touch you very lightly on the forehead the tape will begin to roll.

Now, can you feel 1980? It's April 1980, Jeff — what is he doing? In fact, you're going to be able to see it very clearly and very vividly and the more clear and vivid you see it, the more clear and vivid it will become. You'll relate it very clearly and accurately and as clearly and accurately as you see and feel it.

[SUBJECT RELATES INCIDENT UNDER HYPNOSIS.]

All right, Jeff, now that you've described all that for us, just relax and go deeper into a very rested and relaxed state. In fact, I'm going to count backwards from three to zero and when I say zero you're going to sink even deeper into that very comfortable and relaxed state. Three, two, one and zero. When I tell you to open your eyes you'll be totally and wide awake and after you open your eyes, you're going to find you're going to feel very comfortable, rested, you will have recall and recollection of everything you've told us here today and should you remember anything else within the next

two weeks, you'll be glad to call the investigating officer or myself and relay this information to us, no matter how insignificant. Also, after you open your eyes and come out of this very comfortable, relaxed state, your mind and your body will be relaxed and you're going to find everything is much more clear to you. In fact, you're going to feel very confident about the information you've given us and you're going to have an excellent grasp of all the information you did relate to us under this very relaxed, resting state. Now, feeling very full of vitality and energy under this relaxed state, open your eyes wide awake, open your eyes.

END OF REPORT

Dr. Bradley Kuhns
Reno Police Department
Behavior Science/Polygraph Section

INVESTIGATIVE HYPNOSIS SUPPLEMENTAL

RPD Case #000626

June 26, 1980
RE: Evans, Dan
    Victim
SUBJ: Assault

Now Dan, I would like you to look at the tip of my finger, right there. I'd like you to keep your head level and follow my finger with your eyes. That's fine, by rolling your eyes up toward my finger you're going to find yourself relaxing still more and more and more. Now, Dan, as you watch my finger, your eyes may begin to water, and may begin to maybe burn a little bit, but that's all right, you're going to find them becoming more comfortable and more relaxed as you listen to my voice and they're going to become even more and more comfortable as soon as you feel that they're ready to close.

And now, Dan, just watch that spot on that fingernail. Observe that fingernail and all its detail, noting the shape and the color of the nail with the light bouncing off of it. Just focus on that fingernail until your eyes become completely tired of it and when your eyes become tired of focusing on that fingernail, Dan, just let your eyes close naturally and gently. Don't try to fight or to keep your eyes open now, Dan. Close them immediately as soon as you feel they are ready to close. When you feel you've focused your eyes enough, shut your eyes gently and naturally and comfortably.

Now, take a deep breath and notice how much more relaxed you feel than when you started. Much, much better, you're

NOTE: Names have been changed for report data and individuals' protection.

160

doing fine, Dan. And now, Dan, as you sit there very comfortably with your head erect, relaxed and your eyes closed, let the mental image come to your mind of that neck becoming very soft and very loose and very limp. Now just improve and enhance that image. Allow your head to roll around in a circle very slowly, that's right, very gently, very easily and very gently and, Dan, as you continue rolling your head around you can feel its weight more and more. Now the neck muscles are getting more loose and more limp, more comfortable and more relaxed. That's fine, now Dan, let your head drift and finish rotating in its most comfortable, most relaxed position. Knowing that right now you're going to drift even more deeply relaxed, ready to go still deeper and deeper at the sound of my voice. You're doing fine, Dan, no sounds inside or outside this room are going to bother you or disturb you in this relaxed state now, and as you feel yourself very dreamy and very drowsy, you're going to drift deeper and still deeper, in fact, right now you can notice it's totally and thoroughly relaxing you as you're drifting down deeper and deeper. Still much deeper into that relaxed state. You may find now that your head is becoming very heavy and tired where it's lying in that relaxed state. It may have a tendency to even drift more toward your chest and if it does, allow it to do so, Dan, in fact you may find right now your entire body wants to relax. And you want to breathe even slower and deeper, and if you do, allow yourself to do so. Allow yourself to do so, Dan, feel yourself drifting down with every breath you're taking now to a very comfortable and very relaxed feeling. I can see now that you're drifting deeper and still deeper and as each moment passes by, Dan, from this moment on, each and every breath you take is going to relax you more and more and carry you deeper into a very sound hypnotic sleep. A very deep sleep. A sound sleep where nothing will bother you, disturb you or even awaken you until I give you a signal to awaken.

And now that you're so relaxed and comfortable, Dan, let that imagination visualize very clearly that favorite safe, secure place that we're going to describe as your own private room. It's that filing room. Now to get into that filing room you have to open that door. And now you can see the door to the filing room that has all the filing cabinets of your memory tucked away. And you're going to open the door and as you open the door to that filing room of the cabinets of Dan Evans' memory, you're going to even be more and more comfortable. And now, Dan, that you're inside the room and see all those filing cabinets, you're going to be very amazed and surprised to find that each one of those filing cabinets has the name of Dan Evans on it. And those are your filing cabinets. Those are all your memories, Dan. Things you remember from your entire life, things that have gotten recorded perhaps from the time that you were put on this earth, all the way up to the present time, this exact moment. Now, find the filing cabinet with the year and the date that we require. The date's right there on the filing cabinet. When you find it this finger that I'm touching right here will automatically — that's fine — and now that we have the filing cabinet pull open the drawer and if you look through the files, there's a manila folder and on the top of that folder it has a specific date and when you find that specific date once again this finger will begin to rise, this finger that I'm touching will begin to rise. Also, in that manila folder now when you open it up you're going to find written notes, there's also a video cassette recording of Dan Evans' life on that specific time if you need it and there's also photographs just like a photo album describing day by day, hour by hour and minute by minute, in fact, Dan, it's an exact and accurate vivid record of everything you've experienced, everything you've perceived and done, everything you have seen and heard or felt on that particular date. And now, Dan, as your arm moves from the arm of the chair to you lap, you're going to have a great desire to begin telling me exactly what you see, what you experienced and what you did on that specific date. In fact, Dan, it's all there in front of you, just begin with a photo album and start at the beginning and describe what's happening to Dan Evans at the Winnemucca Police Department. [SUBJECT DESCRIBES EVENTS OF JUNE 26.]

And now, Dan, that you've described what happened on that specific date you're going to find you're going to have extremely vivid recall after I tell you to open your eyes. After this hypnotic session you're going to remember everything you've told me and the investigators during this state of hypnosis. And within the next three or four days should you remember anything that pertains to this issue and what you've told us here today you're going to have a great, great desire to call the investigating officer and relate that information to him, no matter how insignificant it may seem to you, you're going to have a great desire to pick up the telephone and call the investigating officer and relate that information to him.

I'm going to count from one to three, Dan, and on the count of three you're going to be totally and wide awake. One, you're going to find yourself very comfortable, two, you may or may not remember everything that was said or done here but it really doesn't matter, you will remember what you want to remember and forget whay you want to forget. You'll be extremely rested and relaxed, extremely clear-headed, full of vim, vigor and vitality. You're going to feel a thousand times better than you have felt in a long, long time. You're going to be extremely clear-headed, physically refreshed and mentally relaxed and now, three, open your eyes.

END OF REPORT

Dr. Bradley Kuhns
Reno Police Department
Behavior Science/Polygraph Section

163

INVESTIGATIVE HYPNOSIS SUPPLEMENTAL

RPD Case #0000 G 80

August 7, 1980
RE: Ann Jacobs
       Victim
SUBJ: Alleged burglary

Now, Ann, you are going to enter this state of hypnosis very easily and very quickly as I described earlier to you, and you are going to enter the state of hypnosis for the reasons of deep relaxation, vivid recall and self control. Now, as you sit there in that chair I am going to place my right index finger on the pulse of your left wrist and I want you to stare directly at the nail of my right index finger and as you are staring at my right index finger, you are going to enter the state of hypnosis very easily, very quickly, very deeply and very soundly. Now I want you to begin counting backwards from 5 to 0 and you are going to find with each count you are going to relax deeper and deeper and become more comfortable and more calm and when you reach "0" you are going to go deep asleep. Now as you count you can count to yourself, Ann. And as you say "5" you are going to feel your breathing going very much deeper, much more gentle, much more rhythmic. In fact, as your breathing changes you can feel your head begin to nod forward and as your head nods forward slightly you are going to feel a heaviness and as you get to 4 — that's right you are going to feel that heaviness in your eye lids and you are going to become more drowsy and more sleepy. Now as you get to 3 you are going to begin to feel every muscle and every nerve and ever fibre in your body relaxing more and more and more. Deeply relaxing now — you are doing fine. Now you can say to yourself, "2" — your

---

NOTE: Names have been changed for report data and individuals' protection.

164

*arms and legs right now are feeling much more relaxed, in
fact your entire body is deeply relaxed now — deeply relaxed.
And finally as you say "1" your eyelids are growing even
heavier and you can notice that breathing becoming more
rhythmic. You are deeply relaxed and now, "0", you are
deep asleep. That is fine, you are deep asleep. Now, Ann,
you are going to find any suggestions and instructions that I
give you are going to flow into your mind, and as they do
you can automatically turn all those suggestions and all
those instructions into a liquid flow. That liquid flow is
going to turn all of your mind images — your mind thoughts
— and all of the mind beliefs that you are going to have will
in turn reinforce all of the images, thoughts and your beliefs,
and Ann, all the images and thoughts and beliefs will become
truly etched and all of my suggestions and instructions are
only for your benefit and all of the suggestions and instructions for your benefit will remain permanently engraved in
those nerve centers of your mind that control all of those
specific desired and requested actions. The next time that I
say "now" you can open your eyes — "NOW" Ann as you sit
there I want you to look down at your hands and they are
loosely clasped now — right in front of you, so imagine now
that your hands are the jaws of a vice — closing together
tighter and tighter, and tighter until soon you are going to
notice signs of a gradual, even perhaps at first an inner
tension developing as your fingers close down steadily tighter
against your hands and eventually those hands are going to
feel as though they are locked like a vice. You cannot open
them, not even when I tell you to try to do so. You will
not be able to open those hands, that's right, pressing down
tighter and tighter — just as though they are locked in place.
And now when I tell you to try to open your hands you will
find that you are not going to be able to do so. Now, Ann,
try — try very hard — and you are going to find that you are
not going to be able to do so. Try to open those hands, Ann.
Harder — that's right you are not going to be able to open*

them — you are doing fine. Sleep, Ann — deep sleep — you are doing fine. Now Ann, you are going deeper into a very relaxed, comfortable sleep. I am going to lightly touch your hands — and as I lightly touch your hands you are going to find that they are going to be able to separate very easily and quickly. Now — that's right — very good. Just relax deeper asleep. Now, Ann, I am going to awaken you and when I awaken you very shortly you are going to feel very refreshed and very calm, serene, comfortable and contented and about a thousand times more relaxed than you have felt for a long time. I am going to count to three and when I reach the count of three you will be wide awake, comfortable, serene and relaxed . . . 1 — beginning to awaken very easily, very slowly. 2 — your eyes just want to open up very slowly — slowly, comfortably and very surely. 3 — wide awake now feeling wonderful, comfortable and relaxed. That's right 1 — 2 — 3.

END OF REPORT

Dr. Bradley Kuhns
Reno Police Department
Behavior Science/Polygraph Section

INVESTIGATIVE HYPNOSIS SUPPLEMENTAL

RPD Case #0000 G 80

August 7, 1980
RE: Ann Jacobs
        Victim
SUBJ: Alleged burglary

Q. Now, Ann, it is July 16, 1980 — I wonder what you can tell me about the Continental Lodge Motel in the City of Reno, Nevada. Remember it is July 16, 1980.

A. We discussed our trip then although it's like I am remembering it but not visualizing it.

Q. That's alright. That is alright, Ann. Now do you remember looking across the hallway at any time from your room and seeing a room number on the door? Can you tell me the room number directly across the hall?

A. I know it was 13 — 13 something.

Q. If that number pops into your mind at a later time, as we are talking here, it will just pop out of your mouth without any problem should you recall that room number at any time while we are talking. Now, Ann, you are leaving the room getting ready to go out to dinner. Let's pick it up there. What are you aware of?

A. Well, it's dusky dark out, we were walking down the hall and the two gals were there, by the first room with the number something 11.

Q. Walking down the hall — are they on the right or left hand side?

A. On my right.

Q. When you first saw the girls can you tell me what they were wearing?

A. They had uniforms — I know that they had uniforms.

Q. What color?

NOTE: *Names have been changed for report data and individuals' protection.*

167

A. White seems to come to mind and also brown. There was also a big, white cart.

Q. *When you walked up to them how close were you to the girls?*

A. It was a narrow hallway and we walked right by them, and they glanced at each other.

Q. *Did they say anything?*

A. NO, no not at all.

Q. *Did you look back at them?*

A. I think I looked back at them with a sideways glance at them.

Q. *Did you see their faces?*

A. Yes, I did. I know I looked right at them. One was on this side of the cart and one was on that side of the cart.

Q. *Was one taller than the other?*

A. They were both short like I am. I thought they were both 20 or 19.

Q. *What would you say they weighed?*

A. Well, no one was heavy — or thin. I think they looked short and medium. They probably weighed less than 120.

Q. *What nationality would they be?*

A. They were both white girls.

Q. *Ok.*

A. And they both had brown hair and they both did not have short hair. It was more like long hair.

Q. *Did anything strike you as unusual about those girls as you walked by?*

A. Just the way 'that they looked at each other. I don't know, it was like — contact that people make when they have a secret between them.

Q. *Now, Ann, if you were shown photographs or pictures do you think you could pick out the person that you can see in your own mind's eye that is any of those maids in the hallway?*

A. I can pick you the two.

Q. *Do you think so?*

A. Yes. I can remember alot although I can't see them visually like on any screen — I can just remember alot.

Q. *Now here is a photographic lineup with miscellaneous pictures of different women. Open your eyes and tell me if you recognize any of the women.*

A. Well, that is Darcey right there.

(Police Investigator asks)

Q. *What number is that?*

A. Number 4.

(Kuhns speaks)
    Number 4.

(Police Investigator asks)

Q. *How many pictures are you looking at?*

A. Eight.

(Kuhns speaks)

Q. *Now, Ann, in a few moments you are going to be wide awake. Before you are totally wide awake I want you to remember that you are going to have a wonderful trip home — you are going to have less anxiety about plane travel, much less than you had coming up here to the City of Reno and you are going to have a great desire to call me in the next few days after you get home and tell me what a pleasant trip you have had returning home and how much more comfortable and relaxed you feel. Now, on three you will be totally and wide awake and be able to talk to me — 1 — 2 — 3.*

A. Was I really hypnotized? I feel good.

Q. *Do you feel very comfortable and relaxed?*

A. Yes.

[LAUGHTER BY POLICE INVESTIGATOR DOROTHY WILLIAMS, DOCTOR KUHNS AND SUBJECT.]

I guess I really was hypnotized. When you told me that my hands would do what they were supposed to do — they did and my eyes felt different. I felt the changes in my hands — and my eyes certainly did feel different. But

169

all through our talk I didn't feel that much different, but I certainly feel good now.

Q. *Ann, do you have any doubts in your mind that that is the person you saw in the hallway of the Continental Lodge in Reno, Nevada on July 16, 1980?*

A. No, that is the person that I saw — that I thought was a maid.

Q. *Thank you. Investigator Williams, do you have any questions?*

(Investigator Williams)

No.

(Kuhns)

Q. *Then I think we should terminate this interview. Now, Ann, close your eyes very briefly and don't open them until I tell you to. I'm going to assure you that you are going to be totally and wide awake so you will be able to enjoy that airplane trip back to California this evening without any axieties, fears or concerns.*

END OF REPORT

Dr. Bradley Kuhns
Reno Police Department
Behavioral Science/Polygraph Section

INVESTIGATIVE HYPNOSIS REPORT

RPD Case #00005 G 80

August 7, 1980
RE: Ann Jacobs
    WFA/Victim
SUBJ: Alleged burglary

On August 7, 1980, at approximately 10:30 a.m., an investigative hypnosis session was adiministered to Ann Jacobs. Ms. Jacobs travelled from Whittier, California, for the express purpose of undergoing hypnotic induction for possible recall in regard to an alleged burglary incident. The hypnosis session was administered at the request of the subject herself, Ann Jacobs. The investigative hypnosis session was conducted by Dr. Bradley Kuhns and the hypnosis session was administered at the Reno Police Department facilities. The purpose of the investigative hypnosis session was to determine if the victim, Ann Jacobs, could recall any details pertaining to incidents and occurrances that were said to have happened on July 16, 1980.

The alleged burglary was said to have occurred on July 16, 1980 at the Continental Lodge Motel in the city of Reno, Nevada. The approximate loss reported by the victim is said to have been twenty-three hundred dollars. The property taken was said to have been miscellancous jewelry pieces.

Prior to any hypnotic induction, a pre-induction session was conducted in which the procedure of the investigative hypnosis session was explained including all the areas that were to be looked into while Ms. Jacobs was in the state of hypnosis. At the same time, the subject had an opportunity to ask and have answered any and all questions pertaining to the entire procedure that was to be undertaken. Present during the procedures of the hypnotic session were: A. Dr.

Bradley Kuhns, Reno Police Department; B. Police Investigator Dorothy Williams, Detective Division, Reno Police Department; C. Subject, herself.

It should be noted that during the hypnosis session additional recall and refreshment of Ms. Jacobs' memory brought about an identification through a photographic lineup supplied and presented by Police Investigator Dorothy Williams, Reno Police Department. Ms. Jacobs identified photograph number four in the lineup which consisted of eight photographs. When Ms. Jacobs completed this identification, she was then awakened with recognized, standard wakeup procedures, at which time she was left with a post-hypnotic suggestion that should she remember anything pertaining to the issue at hand, no matter how insignificant it seemed to her, she was to contact the investigating officer handling the case and relay all the information to the investigating officer.

After Ms. Jacobs was brought out of the hypnotic state, a brief post-test session was conducted during which time she was allowed to become fully awake and cognizant of her surroundings. She was then excused and she returned to the company of her husband for the trip back to Whittier, California.

Dr. Bradley Kuhns
Reno Police Department
Behavior Science/Polygraph Section

INVESTIGATIVE HYPNOSIS SUPPLEMENT

RPD Case #0000 F 80

June 30, 1980
RE: DUNN, Jean
    WFA-18
    Victim

Now, Jean, just sit on that chair and relax, and for a moment just look straight ahead. You are doing fine, take a deep breath, hold it — hold it for me, now let it out very slowly. You are doing fine. You are doing fine. Now as you let the breath out slowly just focus your eyes up at the ceiling where the wall meets the ceiling. That is right, right in that corner. Just listen to my voice. You are doing fine. I am going to count from 10 to 0. As I say "0" your eyes will become very heavy and very tired and you will sink into a very relaxed state. 10 — your eyelids are becoming just a little bit heavier. 9 — you are doing fine, Jean. 8 — you are relaxing still deeper, your breathing is changing. 7 —, 6 —, when I say 5 you are just going to relax still deeper and your eyes will want to close and if they close before I get to 0 — if they close before I say 0 — just let them close on their own. 5 — 4 — that is alright, now just let those eyes stay closed — they are closed, just let them stay closed. 3 — just waiting for me to say 0 — you are doing fine. 2 — 1 — and 0. Just relax still deeper. Let that breath still take you deeper now. You are doing fine, Jean, just wonderful. Now I want you to see in your mind's eye, I would like you to see in your mind's eye that book that you have been reading at the library. That book that you told me about earlier that you were reading for your class. I want you to see it in your mind's eye and when you do, this finger that I am touching on your right hand will rise in the

---

NOTE: Names have been changed for report data and individuals' protection.

air for me, that's great, Jean, and now that you see the book, now that you see that book in front of you lying there on that library table, I want you to begin leafing through that book. You are going to be surprised and amazed, Jean, as you leaf through that book you will find that when you come to page 119, when you came to page 119 you are going to see the time which will be 5:00 a.m. June 21, 1980 — Now I want you to go back with me as I touch you lightly on the hand — in that one spot that I touched you before — you will begin leafing through those pages in that book and when you reach page 119 you will see the figure 5:00 a.m. And when you reach page 119 and it is 5:00 a.m. June 21, you are going to find your head nod just a little closer to your chest and you are going to be able to tell me what you are doing. Now, Jean, your head just nodded a little deeper towards your chest, so now you can tell me what you are aware of, can't you?

A. Yes. The t.v. screen is there . . . but, it's 11:30 p.m. I see it on t.v.

Q. *What are you aware of, Jean? What time of evening is it?*

A. 11:30 p.m.

Q. *What are you aware of?*

A. I went into the bedroom, got undressed and went to bed.

Q. *Ok, now when you went to bed, did you have any clothing on?*

A. No.

Q. *Now we are going to speed up the film. You will find that you will be able to tell me very vividly and clearly what you were aware of at approximately 5 in the morning. When I touch you lightly on the hand you will be able to describe what you are aware of. Now what are you aware of?*

A. Someone is going through my drawers.

Q. *You are doing fine. It will become more clear and vivid as we go along. Don't worry about losing anything — remember we can speed up the film and slow it down, even*

174

zoom in and freeze any frame to make it more clear and vivid as you would recall the incident. In fact, you will be able to describe it just as though you were watching a blow-by-blow fight on television.

A. He is watching me. He walked over and pulled back my blankets. (SUBJECT BECOMES EMOTIONAL AND BEGINS TO BREATHE VERY HEAVILY — AND SLIGHT TEARING.)

Q. *It is quite alright — you are perfectly safe and secure.*

A. I tried to get away. He is grabbing and choking me harder and harder. (SUBJECT HAS SLIGHT DIFFICULTY IN BREATHING, TRYING TO CATCH HER BREATH.)

Q. *That is alright, you are doing fine — you are perfectly alright. You are safe and secure.*

A. He put his whole arm around me and kept choking harder and harder. I felt a tingling all through my head. I said, "What are you going to do?" He said, "I'm going to f - - - you, can you handle that?" He unzipped his pants — all I could see was his cowboy boots.

Q. *You are doing fine. You are doing fine. Now we are going to reverse the film and go back to the first time that you saw him. Now we have reversed the tape and he is walking over to the bed. What part of his body did you see? What are you aware of?*

A. He is smiling.

Q. *Now you are going to be surprised and amazed — that you are going to be able to see him very clearly and plainly even though you did not have your contacts in that night. Watch how clear and vivid that image becomes as you begin to describe it. It will be as though you had your contacts in and could see him as clearly and plainly as ever. In fact as I touch you lightly on the shoulder you are going to drift deeper than you were before and your mind will become more clear and vivid about the incident.*

A. He has a Boston type accent.

Q. *You are doing fine — I am proud of you.*

175

A. He has his hands around my neck and he is choking me.

Q. *Where would this be? Would it be on the floor — on the bed — where?*

A. On the bed.

Q. *Are you looking at him?*

A. Yea.

Q. *What do you see when you look at him, what part of his body?*

A. His face.

Q. *Ok, you are doing fine. Now let's freeze that frame as you look at his face. Now (a click of the finger and a touch on the hand). You are doing fine — we are going to freeze that face — it's not going to go anywhere now — it can do nothing but get clearer and more vivid as we talk about it. We have all the time in the world. We can relax deeper and deeper and become more accurate as we go along. Now can you see his face clearly?*

A. Sorta.

Q. *That is quite alright, you are doing even better. It will become more clear and vivid even as you describe it to me. Alright now the face is actually frozen there on that screen. It's frozen on that screen and will not go anywhere — now just look at the forehead. Now, after you visualize the forehead look at the overall structure of the face and you tell me what he looks like. For example, it is round, square, oval, octagonal — you tell me.*

A. Sort of a round face.

Q. *That is fine, now look up at his forehead, by his hair line — how would you describe his forehead to me?*

A. His hair is kind of drooping down.

Q. *Alright then, let's talk about his hair — let's talk about his hair for awhile. What about his hair?*

A. It's messed up.

Q. *That's fine. You are doing fine — now you are going to be able to use your hands and fingers as well as your voice to describe and display things for me — it will become very natural and comfortable for you to do that. Now does the hair come down to a certain point or area? You can point it out and show me.*

A. It looks like there is a crease right here kinda.

Q. *Where is that crease?*

A. Right here. (POINTING WITH HER RIGHT HAND TO HER FOREHEAD.) It is like this right here — it's bigger here and smaller over here. (POINTING IN THE AREA OF HER FOREHEAD DESCRIBING THE CREASE.)

Q. *Now look at this . . .*

A. And his eyebrows stick up a little bit right here.

Q. *That's fine. Now look at his hair once again. Does his hair come down to his ears, cover his ears, what — you tell me.*

A. His hair is short. You can see his ears.

Q. *What part of the ear can you see — the earlobe, bottom of the ear, top of the ear — what?*

A. His whole ear. His hair is cut like that. (SUBJECT POINTING TO CERTAIN AREAS OF THE HAIR ON THE LEFT HAND SIDE.) And it is short in the back. (SUBJECT POINTING TO THE BACK OF THE HEAD.)

Q. *That is fine, now let's look at the man's eyes. Usually when a person confronts you the first thing that you see is his mouth and eyes. Now let's look at his eyes — tell me what you are aware of.*

A. They are brown.

Q. *Uh, huh, now do they point in any direction such as up or down or sideways or oval?*

A. The eye sort of goes up and then comes down — more of an almond shape.

Q. *How about the bottom of the eye? Look at the bottom of the eye —*

A. His eyes look kinda normal but he has short eyelashes.

Q. *Where do his eyebrows come to? Can you tell me if he has any hairs in between the eyes?*

A. He has reddish kind of eyes.

Q. *Reddish?*

A. Kind of reddish – like bloodshot.

Q. *Look where his eyebrows come together. Is there any hair there or is it clean? You tell me.*

A. Not too much.

Q. *Now we are going to zoom in on that picture – just the eyes you are going to look at – they will fill up the whole screen. Just those eyes. As I touch you lightly on that one spot we are going to zoom. Now ... (SNAP OF THE FINGER) can you tell me anything about his eyes now?*

A. No, not much more. (SUBJECT TAKES A LONG, LONG DEEP BREATH AND RELAXES DEEPER.)

Q. *You are doing even better, just relax even deeper and it will become more clear and vivid and you will be able to describe even more detail as you remember it. Now let's look at his nose.*

A. It is not really big, kind of a hump. It comes down straight with a little hump. (SUBJECT POINTS TO APPROXI-MATELY THE CENTER OF THE NOSE.) The nose does not look really thin or not too big.

Q. *Can you see his nostrils?*

A. A little.

Q. *You are doing fine – as I told you earlier. You will be able to recall all this information at a moment's notice should we require it. In fact later on the police artist will finish out all this detail you are giving me now. You will be surprised and amazed that you will be able to recall all that you are telling me now very easily. Now let's just look at that over-all face once again. How close is his face to you?*

A. He is very close.

Q. *Can you see anything such as any facial hair at all?*

A. He looks clean shaven. No moustache or beard. He has little ears.

Q. *Little ears? How are they shaped?*

A. They come out (POINTING TO HER LEFT EAR) and are sort of rounded here.

Q. *Can you see an earlobe?*
A. It does not have one like mine. It's connected like grown in.
Q. *Now about his cheeks.*
A. Sort of high cheekbones.
Q. *Ok, now can you see his complexion?*
A. He has whiskers.
Q. *What about his whiskers?*
A. They are right here. (POINTING TO THE LEFT AND RIGHT SIDE OF HER CHEEKS.) I can feel them when he rubs them against me. (SUBJECT STARTS TO CRY VERY LIGHTLY AND HER VOICE BECOMES EMOTIONAL.)
Q. *That is quite alright — you are doing fine — you are safe and secure and you will continue to be so as long as you are here in this room. Now you said you watched him when he smiled. Look at his lips — how do they look to you — would you say that the bottom is bigger than the top or are they the same size or is there something unusual about them — you tell me.*
A. The bottom lip is a little bigger than the top but not too much.
Q. *Are you aware of any crease between the nose and the lip?*
A. Yes, there is.
Q. *Now scan his chin — look at his chin — what can you tell me about his chin and jaw? What do they look like?*
A. His chin is not really to a point and it's not square. His chin is sort of round and there is a crease, I see a crease — right there (SUBJECT POINTING TO LOWER PART OF THE CHIN).
Q. *That's great, you are doing fine. Now just look at that face a little closer — is there anything on the face such as cuts, bruises, anything that you can tell me that is unusual about that face?*
A. No.

Q. *Are you aware of any odors that came from that man?*

A. No. He seemed clean. It was like, it was like he just brushed his teeth or something.

Q. *Ok, now did you see his teeth?*

A. They were sharp — like you could see his eye teeth. (SUBJECT POINTS WITH HER LITTLE FINGER TO HER LEFT EYE TOOTH.)

Q. *That's fine.*

A. I can see a crease. I can really see a crease right there. (SUBJECT POINTS TO THE LEFT SIDE OF HER MOUTH.) I can see a crease when he smiles.

Q. *That is fine. I am proud of you. Now look at his head as it sits on his shoulders. Some people have all different shapes of necks. You tell me what you are aware of.*

A. (SUBJECT BECOMES SLIGHTLY EMOTIONAL.) You can see his neck muscles. (SHE POINTS TO THE NECK MUSCLES ON THE LEFT SIDE OF HER NECK.) He's kind of thin. In fact he is kind of thin in the cheeks. He has high cheek bones — you can see kinda shallow cheeks. His smile is not like a big smile.

Q. *That is fine — you are doing fine. Now let's just back off so that you can view his whole body. Now when I touch you lightly on the hand we are going to have that scene of his whole body. Now how tall would you say that he is if you had to compare him to somebody. In your own words.*

A. He is taller than me — but not really big. He was not real skinny at all. His legs were not really skinny but not muscular — not real heavy at all. About 5-10 or so.

Q. *That is fine — you are doing just fine. Now on the count of three you are going to open your eyes. And the second time I count three you are going to close your eyes and sink even deeper. (10 times) even more than you are now. 1-2-3. (SNAP OF THE FINGERS.) That's right — you are doing fine. 1-2-3 (SNAP). Deep sleep. Deep sleep. Now you saw those boots. What color are they?*

180

A. They are black. And they have silver tips on them.

Q. *That is fine — now what color is his shirt?*

A. Brown with a pocket right here. (SUBJECT POINTS TO THE LEFT HAND SIDE OF THE CHEST.)

Q. *Do you notice anything else about his clothing that seems unusual?*

A. He is wearing like a pouch — a leather pouch on his left side. It jingles — like he has tools in it.

Q. *Jean, now that you are seeing the incident from a distance full view — let's review what he did.*

A. He bent over the bed — he choked me. I pulled away and just about got away.

Q. *Go on.*

A. As I started to get away — he got me on the floor. He bent me over — doggie fashion. I was on my hands and knees.

Q. *Ok.*

A. Then he said, "I'm going to f - - - you." (SUBJECT BE-COMES EMOTIONAL AND BEGINS TO CRY.)

Q. *It's quite alright — you are safe and secure — you will be alright. You are seeing it without any physical contact.*

A. I hear him taking down his pants. I hear the things in his pockets jingling — I'm facing the floor.

Q. *Go on.*

A. He put it in my vagina — and my rectum. He switches on and off. He just did it — he put it in both — he is trading off.

Q. *Ok.*

A. He took a pillow case and he wrapped it around my face — I could see light but I could not see much else. It was over my whole face but when I looked down I could see part of his body.

Q. *Go on, Jean.*

A. He took me back to the bed. He did it again in the bed.

Q. *How did he do it?*

A. He did it again in the vagina and the rectum. He stuck a

pillow up underneath me and a pillow case over my head like I was not a real person. He treated me like nothing.

Q. *Now was the pillow case completely over your head on the bed?*

A. Only partly. It came down to about here. (SUBJECT POINTING TO APPROXIMATELY THE BRIDGE OF THE NOSE. SUBJECT CRYING.)

Q. *You are doing fine — everything will be alright — you are safe — very safe. After he did it to you that time on the bed what happened?*

A. After he did it he fell asleep. After I thought he was asleep for awhile I got away, and ran out of bed.

Q. *And then what happened?*

A. He woke up and grabbed me by the hand and started to take me to the other room. I broke away and ran outside and began to scream.

Q. *And then what happened?*

A. And then he ran away.

Q. *Just go deeper — just relax deeper. Now Jean — you are going to see that man's face again. Very clearly — and when you see it as clearly as you did before — when you see that man's face as clearly as you did before — this finger that I am touching on your hand will begin to rise. This finger will rise up into the air when you see his face as clearly as before. (SUBJECT'S RIGHT FINGER RISES INTO THE AIR.) That is fine, you are doing great, Jean. You are doing great. Now look at that face again, Jean. What we are going to do is transpose that face from your mind — that description you gave us earlier from your mind onto a piece of paper. The police artist that is sitting in this room will now finish out the detail of that description that you gave me earlier. Do you understand?*

A. Yes.

Q. *Now in a few moments I will have you open your eyes. As you open your eyes you are going to find yourself in a deep state of hypnosis — in fact as you open your eyes you are going to sink deeper — but you will be aware of that picture in your mind and you are going to be able to look at the sketch that the police artist already has drawn and you will make corrections and the corrections will be as clear and as vivid and as accurate as the picture that you have now retained in that memory of yours. Now Jean, that picture that you have already locked in your memory, that you have described for me earlier and you are going to once again describe to this police artist — do you think if you saw that man right now you would be able to recognize him?*

A. Yes, definitely.

Q. *That is fine. In a few moments I am going to count to three and on the count of three — you will open your eyes and sink deeper into a very comfortable state of hypnosis but be fully capable of correcting the drawing that you will see in front of you. 1-2-3-. Now that you have recalled all that vital information you can feel assured in your mind that whatever happened to you will never make you any other person but the good person that you really are. You know now in your own mind that because something traumatic may have happened to you it will not change the good person that you are inside. You have been a good person all of your life and you will continue to be so. I think now that you will find that your reviewing this thing in your own mind with me here today will enable you to see things much more clearly in such a light that you can understand now that things happen to people in this world, but that does not mean that life cannot go on. You are going to have the feeling of well-being and comfort knowing that you can understand what happened with a much easier mind, knowing now that you can go on with your life and be the person that you have always wanted to be. Now, Jean, I am going to awaken you very shortly — I am going to count to three. On the count of three you will be totally and wide awake*

183

feeling wonderful, feeling calm, feeling secure, knowing that things will work out for you for the better. I will be awakening you very shortly and after I awaken you, you will find yourself going to be very refreshed, very comfortable, contented, and relaxed. Now I shall count to three. When I reach the count of three you will be wide awake, refreshed, comfortable, contented and relaxed. 1 — beginning to awaken, 2 — eyes opening slowly and surely, 3 — wide awake feeling wonderful and relaxed, feeling wonderful and relaxed. Isn't that a good feeling now? Isn't that a good feeling?

END OF REPORT

Dr. Bradley Kuhns
Reno Police Department
Behavior Science/Polygraph Section

Rape victim under hypnosis assists police artist with composite drawing.

INVESTIGATIVE HYPNOSIS REPORT

RPD Case #0000 F 80

July 1, 1980
RE: Dunn, Jean
      WFA, 18 years
      Victim
SUBJ: Sexual Assault

On July 1, 1980 at approximately 6:30 P.M. an investigative hypnosis session was administered to the above named subject. This session was administered at the request of Officer Jerry Hazen, Detective Division, Reno Police Department. The investigative hypnosis session was conducted by Dr. Bradley Kuhns and the hypnosis session was administered at the Reno Police Department facility. The purpose of this investigative hypnosis session was to determine if any additional information could be retrieved from the subject to assist the Reno Police Department in their on-going investigation pertaining to the issue at hand — the issue at hand being sexual assault. Prior to any hypnotic inductions, a pre-induction session was conducted in which the procedures of the investigative hypnosis session were explained, including all the areas that were to be looked into while the subject was in the state of hypnosis. At the same time this subject had an opportunity to ask and have answered any and all questions pertaining to the entire procedure that was to be undertaken. In addition, prior to any hypnotic inductions a consent and release waiver was obtained from the subject. The information sought from victim, Dunn, was possible identification by means of a composite drawing of the suspect that committed the sexual assault upon her person. Further, any identification of the suspect that the victim should recall. Persons present during the investigative hypnosis session were: A.) Dr.

NOTE: Names have been changed for report data and individuals' protection.

185

Bradley Kuhns, Reno Police Department; B.) Police Artist, Reno Police Department; C.) Subject, Jean Dunn, victim.

Recognized inductions and standard techniques were utilized and the following information was elicited from the victim while under hypnosis:

A. The victim, Dunn, was awakened by a noise approximatey five a.m. on June 21, 1980. The individual suspect then approached the victim's bed and advised her he was going to have sex with her. When victim Dunn refused, the suspect beat and choked the victim, Dunn, until she agreed to submit to his sexual advances.

B. The suspect was said to have put a pillow case over the victim's head.

C. The suspect then placed the victim on the floor and sexually assaulted her by committing acts of vaginal and anal intercourse.

D. The victim stated the suspect committed vaginal/anal intercourse while he had the victim on the floor, then the suspect placed the victim on the bed wherein he had vaginal/anal intercourse with the subject again.

E. The sexual attack on the victim was described to have lasted for a period anywhere from 45 minutes to an hour and a half.

S.D.I. (SUSPECT DESCRIPTION INFORMATION):

A. The victim described the suspect as approximately five-ten to six feet tall.

B. "The hair was not too long, and dark."

C. The suspect was described as wearing an orange shirt, possibly resembling a T shirt with a pocket over the left breast area.

D. Wearing jeans.

E. Cowboy boots, described as dark, possibly black with silver tips.

F. The victim described the suspect as a white male adult

between the ages of 20 and 25.

G. The victim states that the suspect was wearing something on his belt that resembled a pouch. She indicated that the pouch was worn on the right hand side of the suspect. Further, she indicated that there was a jangling and rattling noise, as if she heard tools in the pouch. The victim described the pouch as brown in color formed in a round sort of manner which had a cover and a clasp attachment on the cover.

MISCELLANEOUS INFORMATON:

The reader is referred to the police artist's composite of the suspect that was obtained from the victim while in a state of hypnosis.

The victim, Dunn, was then awakened with recognized and standard wake-up procedures, at which time she was left with a post-hypnotic suggestion that should she recall anything pertaining to the issue at hand she would contact the investigating officer handling the case and relay all the information she recalls to that investigating officer. After Dunn was brought out of the hypnotic state a brief post-test session was conducted during which time she was allowed to become fully awake and aware of her surroundings. She also stated that she now had full recall of what was said and done in the state of hypnosis. Further, the victim, Dunn, indicated she had a much better feeling of well-being and understanding of the situation and felt that she could cope much more easily now that she had undergone a hypnotic session. She was then excused and the investigative hypnosis session was concluded.

END OF REPORT

Dr. Bradley Kuhns
Reno Police Department
Behavior Science/Polygraph Section

CHAPTER V
American Institute of Hypnosis

7188 SUNSET BOULEVARD / LOS ANGELES, CALIFORNIA 90046

Special Award and Commendation

This special award and commendation is presented to:

DR. BRADLEY WILLIAM KUHNS

who has distinguished himself for many years in the fields of Naturopathics, Psychophysiology, Psychotheraputics, Hypnotherapy and Hypnosis in Medicine. He is the author of papers on the subjects. He has done original research with hypnosis and polygraph and has given freely of his time and energy for the benefit of hundreds of patients and for the benefit of the AMERICAN INSTITUTE OF HYPNOSIS and the AMERICAN COLLEGE OF MEDICAL HYPNOTISTS. He has taught many doctors the use of hypnosis in their practice throughout the United States at various courses given by the AMERICAN INSTITUTE OF HYPNOSIS and sponsored by the AMERICAN COLLEGE OF MEDICAL HYPNOTISTS. He has also given proof of participation in teaching and studies abroad through numerous workshops.

For his excellence in practice, teaching and service, this Special Award and Commendation is presented to:

DR. BRADLEY WILLIAM KUHNS, F.I.A.H., F.A.C.M.H.

Date of This Award: May 26, 1975

The Daily Report Ontario, California Oct. 8, 1979

Doctor conquers pain with hypnosis

By ROBERT LEE
Staff Writer

Most people would be uncomfortable at the thought of spending three hours in the dentist's chair. Doing it without anesthesia would be impossible.

Virginia Hawkins of Upland went through such a procedure using hypnosis as her only anesthesia.

Mrs. Hawkins explained that her fear of dentists is such that she has in the past avoided going to them, bitten them or thrown up on them. To complicate her fear of dentists, she has an allergic reaction to most anesthetics.

But she said she reme bers nothing of her most recent trip to the dentist to have seven teeth capped and chooses not to remember anything.

Using hypnosis as an anesthetic has been around since 1840, but the medical professions have only recently recognized its value as a medical tool.

According to Dr. Bradley Kuhns, Mrs. Hawkins' hypnotherapist, using hypnosis is often the only substitute where a patient cannot take a great deal of anesthesia or where, as in the case of Mrs. Hawkins, the person has an inordinate amount of fear.

Dr. John Entner, Mrs. Hawkins' dentist, said "Most of the time I feel a lot of hostility and aggression from patients. People hate the dentist and don't like going to him."

But of his recent work on Mrs. Hawkins, he said, "It was as easy as anyone I've worked with. It would be nice if everyone were trained to do this so they wouldn't have to hang onto the chair."

Dr. Kuhns said dentistry provides an excellent opportunity for the medical application of hypnosis.

"Once they're under they don't care if they ever get up. It's the greatest high in the world," said Dr. Kuhns.

He described the procedure as that of "short circuiting" the brain's sensory perception and relaxing the patient.

He added that the hypnotic state, which has been described as a sleep or trance-like state, is actually a state of of heightened awareness.

"Your mind's more clear, but nothing bothers you," he said. "The pain is still there, we just block it out.

"We relate to things people know," he added. "People know the effects of Novocain so when I say your jaw is going to become as cold and as numb as it did the last time at the dentist's the mind can relate to it."

Dr. Entner, who has had some limited hypnosis training, said the pain people associate with dentists is one of the hardest things to deal with.

"When a person comes to see a

dentist he's normally frightened," said Dr. Entner. "And if the dentist says something is going to hurt then it will hurt all that much more. Pain is a two-part thing: what actually happens to the nerve, which is a very mechanical thing, and then there is the perception of pain."

He added that fear will heighten the pain.

In the case of Mrs. Hawkins, he said, the fear was such that without the hypnosis the dental work she had done would have probably have had to have been done in a hospital.

"If I were to have this done on myself it would have been traumatic," said Dr. Entner. "For Virginia it would have been impossible."

Dr. Kuhns commented, "Fear is one of the biggest things dentists have to fight. They have the highest suicide rates of any medical profession in the world because of the tension. That's why you always see young dentists."

Mrs. Hawkins said her first experience with a dentist, when she was 5, probably programmed her feelings towards the profession.

"I had to have a tooth filled," she explained. "The dentist gave me nothing for the pain and I was crying. He got mad and I can remember him holding me in the chair and lecturing me."

She said since that time she has viewed dentists as some of the most insensitive of medical practitioners.

But, Dr. Kuhns said hypnosis is not a panacea and not everyone could go through the procedure as Mrs. Hawkins did without some form of anesthesia.

"A competent hypnotist will tell you that hypnosis is not a cure-all," said Dr. Kuhns. He said that although he believes everyone can be hypnotized, not everyone can be hypnotized to the same degree.

He added that when he goes to the dentist he has a light anesthesia besides using self-hypnosis.

And Dr. Entner said that hypnosis, although a useful tool in treating difficult patients, probably will not replace the anesthesia used today.

"Most people tolerate the dental procedure quite well," he said, estimating that drugs are effective in better than 90 percent of patients.

But for the few who have problems, Dr. Entner said, it could prove to be a boon.

A SEMANTIC "SHOPPING LIST" FOR HYPNOTISTS

LET IT GO	WONDERFUL FEELING
BE AT EASE	INDIFFERENT
TRANQUIL	DETACHED
PEACEFUL	NUMB
CALM	SUBLIME
MAKE YOURSELF COMFORTABLE	REPOSE
RELEASE YOUR TENSIONS	WORRY FREE
SERENE	LETHARGIC
A FEELING OF WELL-BEING	SOFTEN

A VIEW PERTAINING TO HUMAN BEHAVIOR

By   Dr. Bradley Kuhns
     F.A.I.H., F.A.C.M.H.

A brief overview

In the field of human behavior as a whole, the contingencies of reinforcement which define operant behavior have clarified the nature of the relation between behavior and its consequences and have devised techniques which apply to the methods of natural science to its investigation.

Basically, there are three principles of reinforcement. They are: (a) positive reinforcement; (b) negative reinforcement; and (c) extinguishing a response. A positive reinforcement will strengthen the response it follows and make that response more likely to occur. A negative reinforcement weakens the response it immediately follows, and, a response is extinguished by withholding reinforcement.

Theories offered are many, and one specific theory is that identifiability reinforces the formation associations. Identifiability is not merely a perceptible difference of one figure from another when the two are side-by-side, but really implies a rememberable difference. Thorndike's "law of effect" was used to describe an act that is closely followed by: (a) satisfaction; (b) pleasure, and (c) comfort, which will be learned. An act that is followed by discomfort is forgotten. Thordike's theories and ideas constitute a theory of association, as distincet from a theory of conditioned responses, in which an association may be between autonomous central processes instead of between afferent and efferent processes.

Hull believes the reinforcing connections involved in learning are: (a) weakened by being activated and need a period of recovery before they can function again; and (b) strengthened when the period of recovery is permitted. Hull calls the weakening influence reactive inhibition and feels behavior is determined by sensory stimulations, therefore, learning consists of forming stimulus-response connections.

Skinner's movement rejects physiological hypothesis. He stresses a method that correlates observable stimuli with observable responses; and recognizing that explanation is ultimately a statement of relationships between observed phenomena. He proposes to have psychology confine itself to such statements now. Skinner also states: "Programed instruction and contingency management in the classroom are products of operant conditioning, and I have an interest in applying operant conditioning principles to government and international affairs." *(Operant Behavior, Honig & Werner, N.Y. 1966)*

An ideal way to study "anticipatory behavior" is to observe its emergence in organisms whose existing repertories lack directed patterns of response. In 1955 a human infant was exposed to a metronome followed by an electric shock to one limb. In the beginnig all four limbs responded to the shock in a generalized way. Repetition brought about a specific "anticipatory response" involving only the shocked limb.

Another situation: A dog was used wherein he was placed in a long shuttle box. Either side of the box could be electrified. A buzzer was sounded for 10 seconds every three or four minutes and each buzz followed by a fairly strong electric shock lasting approximately one half minute. The animal began avoiding the shock by crossing over to the unelectrifed compartment during the signal before the onset of the shock.

The generalization arrived at from the two mentioned behaviors were: (a) Some degree of repeated exposure to a situation is a necessary condition for the development of activities that are anticipatory with respect to some feature of that situation, and (b) it appears that behavior becomes anticipatory when certain responses that are accompanied by a *given goal* are *selectively reinforced*. The increase in anticipatory movements appears to constitute an integrated goal-directed response.

At this point let us consider an emotional disturbance such as fear. Fear may be arranged into three classes of responses: (1) A source of emotion; fear of the strange can be operationally demonstrated by a chimp reared in total darkness. The fear is not innate since the animal reared in the darkness does not show it until vision in general has begun to have some meaning for him and it arouses phase sequences. A familiar attendant wearing the familiar coat of another attendant may arouse fear as a complete stranger would. (First attendant causes no disturbance, nor does the second,) but first and second attendant together causes a violent emotional reaction.

It is this fact that makes it necessary to suppose that two phase-sequences may interfere with one another. This class of motional disturbance thus is one caused by a conflict which may be extended to the disruptive effect of pain stimuli. (2) Fear of the dark, solitude and fear aroused by loss of support follow prolonged absence of normal auditory stimulation. It appears that it would also comprise emotional disturbance due to contact with a dead body which lacks the usual responsiveness, anger at a lack of social response in another person, grief, homesickness, etc. (3) Emotional changes are frequently associated with intracranial tumors, compression of blood vessels, asthma, vascular disease that acts to produce vascular spasm in intracranial vessels. The amount of oxygen supplying the neural tissues is lessened and it can be assumed that emotional disturbance is a disruption of timing of neuronal activity, in the cerebrum.

This, more than likely, accounts for the incoordinations of emotions. It appears that the coodinated part of emotional behavior with unpleasant emotions has one constant function: to put an end to the original stimulation.

It certainly appears that strong emotional distubances such as fear tend to prevent the repetition of any line of thought that leads up to it and to eliminate the corresponding behavior.

McClelland's theory and study incorporate motivation. *(Understanding Human Motivation, World Publishing Co., 1965)* This theory offers three hypotheses: (1) The method of measurement for maximum theoretical usefulness was to be at least partially independent of the methods of measurement used to define the other two main variables in contemporary psychological theory, namely perception and learning; (2) It was assumed that motives might be best measured in fantasy. This was felt as true because: (a) fantasy fills the first requirement. It differs from problem solving behavior on the one hand and the veridical perception on the other; and (b) clinical psychologists have found fantasy of value in developing the motivational theory of personality. (3) It was felt that motives could be experimentally aroused by manipulation (manipulating external conditions).

McClelland used human subjects deprived of food for 1, 4 and 16 hours who then wrote five minute stories in response to each of four pictures exposed for 20 seconds. The questions asked about the pictures were: What is happening? What has led to this situation? What is being thought? What will happen? Instructions given were standard ones for "Thematic Apperception Tests." The general results of his research were:

1. The demonstration of the potentials of an achievement score based on fantasy.

2. By providing an independent measure of motivation, it has opened up areas in the relations between achievement motivation and school grades.

3. The demonstration that the method of deriving a measure of motivational strength from experimentally produced changes such as fantasy is a practical one.

It should be noted that reflexes, releasing processes, orientation responses, etc., belong in the category of response-eliciting stimuli or impinging on the organism, representing information on environment being received by the (animal/human).

These processes achieve an instantaneous adaptation of behavior to the environmental requirements of the moment. They are not, or do not, cause a modification in the mechanism of the response but are themselves the function of highly differentiated adaptive mechanisms. It should also be noted that the fixed action patterns depending on endogenous production of excitation, particularly those which occur rarely

in the (animal/human) life such as fighting or activities belonging to the reproductive cycle are very sensitive to bad rearing and respond to it by a quantitative decrease.

PHYSIOLOGICAL FUNCTIONS OF THE BRAIN AND BODY

By **Dr. Bradley Kuhns**
   F.A.I.H., F.A.C.M.H.

Reprinted from the *California Association of Polygraph Examiners* Newsletter
Winter 1979

An insight into brain-psychophysiology

In theory, everything anyone has ever seen, done, or heard in his lifetime is stored and recorded forever in the brain. Granted, one may not instantaneously recall everything which he has experienced in a lifetime, but it is there, nonetheless. Let us divide one section of the brain into two separate sections. We shall call one section "conscious memory" and the other section we shall call the "unconscious memory."

A person's ability to recall something from the past is always present. If an individual could see the responses of another charted on a physiological recorder such as a polygraph, or an EEG printout, it would be quite evident that recall is ever present and on-going. Reactions are often noted that are explainable by recall. For example, a thinking response begins, and it does not stop until the answer comes. An experience meeting an old friend, being unable to recall his or her name may explain this phenomenon. If one thinks about the forgotten name seriously enough, perhaps within a few hours, or perhaps after a good

night's sleep, he will suddenly recall the name.

The medulla oblongata

Another section of the brain known as the "medulla of the brain stem" (medulla oblongata) automatically controls certain functions of the body which include breathing, heart rate, pulse rate, increases and decreases of blood pressure and expansion and contraction of the arteries. The average male breathes 14 - 18 cycles per minute with the average female breathing somewhat faster. The medulla oblongata is the hindmost and lowest part of the brain which narrows down into the spinal cord.

The hypothalamus

The hypothalamus is the organ that receives a "complex pattern" of afferent connections from higher brain areas such as the limbic system. Furthermore, the hypothalamus acts as a mobilizer of energy to deal with certain emergencies, as well as other human or autonomic functions, not to mention the regulation of hunger and sexual activity. Certain system structures (limbic in nature) serve to connect the hypothalamus and the cortex through "two-way" neural pathways. These pathways are "reverberating circuits" of "feedback mechanisms" which allow the reciprocity of connection. Most scientists agree that the hypothalamus is the "clearing-house of emotions." In fact, it may be assumed that the hypothalamus is the mediator of emotions. Such autonomic responses like rising blood pressure, sweaty palms, blushing, pallor, and so on, are routine. but there are other responses which distinctly involve striated muscle which provide responses like fear, rage, (or the trembling of rage) and facial grimaces. Then, in another part of the brain, we have what I would describe as two computers. I'm referring to the "hypothalamus" and the "limbic system." The so-called computers act as protective devices for the human body. Two sets of nerve fibers pass through these two computers. One set is called "motor nerves" and the other set is called "sensory nerves." Motor nerve fibers pass impulses from the brain out to all parts of the body. Sensory nerve fibers, on the other hand, receive the impulses from all parts of the body and transmit them to the brain. All of these nerve fibers, both motor and sensory, pass through the "computer" section of the brain. Two computers work closely together to keep body functions in a sort of "balance" which is known as homeostasis. When body functions go out of balance, or while homeostasis is being lost, changes or physiological reactions and responses occur. Homeostatic centers are placed abundantly around the third and fourth ventricles, and they react to neocortically directed activities especially during physical work or concentrated cognitive work as well as when one voluntarily induces himself to relax, as in self-hypnosis.

The limbic system

The limbic system is to the feeling states what the reticular system is to somatovisceral adjustments. Structurally, the limbic system makes up the inner core of the brain concealed by the convolutions of the neocortex or the "new brain." Experimental evidence indicates very strongly that this older structure could possibly serve as a "nonspecific activator" for the cortex itself, which would facilitate or inhibit learning, memory, external behavior as well as internal feelings. On another level, the limbic system allows visceral bodily needs to be given expression, and purely ideational functions are secondary. The limbic system interprets experience through giving meaning to experience instead of utilizing symbols that are produced intellectually. In addition to its effectiveness in mediating subjective emotional experiences, the limbic system correlates primitive motivational and emotional processes. The limbic system exerts very great power or control and it is often referred to as an "automatic pilot" so the outside world and the visceral (inside world) of the individual can become integrated.

The cerebellum

Then there is the part of the brain known as the cerebellum. Here all muscle coordination takes place to include the development of "learned reactions." For example, when a baby is born, he cannot walk or talk. As the baby grows older and normally, he learns to do both of these tasks rather automatically. He does not need to concentrate while walking up a street, for example, to move one foot forward and then the other. It is a fact that one can be concentrating on other matters and actually be unaware of his mechanical walking movements. Driving a vehicle is another good example. There is similarly a vast number of muscles required simply to answer a question with a simple "yes" or "no." Yet, after one has learned to talk, he does not concentrate on when or how he must move his diaphragm, lungs, throat muscles, jaw, tongue and lips. If one decides to answer a question "yes" or "no" the mechanics come more or less automatically. This is another example of learned reaction.

Data processing

Compare intelligence and judgment of the human brain with that of a lower animal such as a dog or a cat. You will find that the human brain is far superior. The lower form does not have the ability or capability to make judgments or decisions in determining future consequences.

One can think of the brain as an information data processing center, the body and mind connected, one being dependent on the other, like a sophisticated computer. The brain is constantly receiving a flow of information from a vast network of nerves. It's called the autonomic nervous system (ANS). That information the brain is receiving allows the person in his own mind to monitor his external and internal environment. And the individual can be aware of all of this at the same time. So, through the eyes, ears, nose, throat, a person can be aware of the environment around him through sense of touch, smell, etc.

Example: If a bright light shines into the eyes, the eyes are going to translate that bright light in terms of a message going to the brain. The brain immediately measures the light intensity, and if the light intensity exceeds the tolerences of the eye or is going to damage the eye, the person is going to get instructions immediately to close his eyes, turn the head away from the light, or possibly squint. But, the body has to do something to avoid the bright light source. Or, as another example, loud noises or bad food. The body will reject the bad food as soon as it touches the tongue, or perhaps even

before if the sense of smell triggers a reaction. The body is constantly monitoring what is going on. And, it is all being monitored by the person while that person goes along through the day, without any specific thought or attention directed to regulation. The individual does not have to think of being hungry, sleepy etc. All functions are governed automatically by the ANS.

The autonomic nervous system

The ANS is subdivided into two divisions; the "sympathetic" and the "parasympathetic." These are the two divisions that work together to maintain the body in the constant form of balance previously discussed, the balance

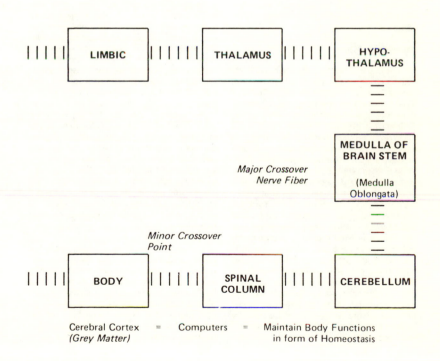

Cerebral Cortex = Computers = Maintain Body Functions
(Grey Matter)   in form of Homeostasis

195

of homeostasis, which is necessary for normal functioning.

    Example: The sympathetic system, wherein the heart is beating very fast due to excitement. It beats harder and faster. If there were nothing to slow the heart action down, it would literally beat out of the person's chest, best described as a tire blowing out. To counter this "blow out," the parasympathetic division initiates impulses that slow the heart down and the fast, beating activity is brought under control and back into a normal balance. This type of up/down activity constantly occurs with a continuous action and always serves as a protective system within the human body.

    Remember, the brain consists of 10 to 15 billion tiny brain cells and each brain cell has the ability to communicate or signal to any one or a thousand other brain cells simultaneously; and this one or thousand brain cells can communicate back with that single cell. A fantastic computer. A data processing center! The cells are so small that hundreds of them can be placed on the point of a pin.

The Cerebral Cortex

    The place where these brain cells are located is call the "cerebral cortex," better known as "grey matter." This is where, in the brain, higher thinking and learning processes take place. Think of a railroad track and a railroad car traveling that track. The track is a nerve fiber, microscopic in size, and this track goes through various "cities" known as the limbic system, the thalamus and part way through the hypothalamus. These then are the computers that maintain the body functions in the form of homeostasis. There are two "nodes" at the base of the thalamus where impulses from the ears enter directly into the thalamic area. Nerve fibers pass on through the "medulla of the brain stem" and, in part, through the cerebellum and out into the body via the spinal column.

    At the base of the medulla oblongata a major cross-over point of nerve fibers for the upper part of the human body occurs and it is for this reason that the left side of the brain controls the right side of the body and vice-versa. At the base of the spinal column there is another minor cross-over point which does the same for the nerve fibers going to the lower extremities.

Electro-chemical reactions

    In understanding the physiology of the body, it should be remembered that there are various chemical reactions taking place in the body at all times. In hypnosis, the operator is basically familiar with "Galvanic Skin Response" or "Galvanic Skin Reflex" (GSR). *(For those unfamiliar with a GSR meter, it may be pointed out that this device is basically activated by the sweat glands.)* Although at times the operator may monitor the GSR with an audible tone, it should be noted that the readings from the visual meter are read with great care and consideration. Remember, such things as thinking activity, subtle inner tensions and body movement will cause stimulation of the sweat glands. In addition to the sweat gland reaction, the trigger could possibly set off other chemical activity relating to possibly the adrenal glands, the chemicals or hormones known as "epinephrine" and "norepinephrine" to be specific. "Norepinephrine" is a crystalline compound and, with epinephrine, has a strong vasoconstriction action. It is only one of 32 chemicals or hormone forms secreted into the human body by the adrenal gland (which is located on top of the kidneys). The constriction caused by the compounds indirectly affect the skin capillaries. The chemical causes "dilation" in other parts of the body. So, basically this writer would suggest that when using a GSR monitor, analysis should be with great care and speculation when it is being utilized as a sole physiological recorder.

    This article was not meant to be a lecture on psychology, as I feel certain most of you have had second year psychology, but rather, it has been a basic look at the physiological function of the brain and body so as to offer a glimmer of understanding on how various things appear and why certain reactions happen as they do.

196

CALVIN R.X. DUNLAP
District Attorney

September 29, 1980

Chief James Parker
Reno Police Department
P. O. Box 1900
Reno, Nevada 89505

Re: <u>State of Nevada vs. Morey Kaplan</u>

Dear Jim:

I would like to take this opportunity to commend a number of your officers and employees for their extremely fine cooperation, assistance and just plain good police work in the above referenced case.

As you know, the whole case was made possible as the result of the confidence which Marge Carter had in Sergeant Kenny Bunker. Kenny has, through the long course of this case, done an extremely fine job of relating to and assisting us with Marge Carter. His diplomacy and instinct for handling this delicate matter was, in a very large measure, responsible for the success we obtained in convicting Morey Kaplan both times.

In addition, I would like to commend Lieutenant Charlie Nearpass and Lieutenant Wayne Lucia for their persistence and detailed work on the case which also contributed in great measure to the conviction of this dangerous killer. Their relentless attention to detail constitutes, in my opinion, extremely fine police work, notwithstanding some of the attacks upon them by the defense.

Detective John Kimpton also contributed greatly to the success of this case with his fine detective work and I am particularly grateful for his assistance regarding the technicalities of the polygraph which became an integral part of the case this time. John was, as usual, extremely responsive and willing to help in every detail.

I would also like to commend and thank Bradley Kuhns for his assistance in putting together for me materials on the subject of hypnosis, which materials were quite important to me in the successful admission of certain testimony by Charlie Daniels.

I would like to commend all of the members of the Reno
Police Department that worked on the case.

Finally, thank you for your cooperation and for allowing me
the use of the necessary manpower and resources of your
Department in order to put away this dangerous killer.

Kindest personal regards,

Sincerely,

CALVIN R. X. DUNLAP
District Attorney

CRXD/jz
cc: Sergeant Kenny Bunker
     Lieutenant Charlie Nearpass
     Lieutenant Wayne Lucia
     Detective John Kimpton
     Detective Bradley Kuhns
     Detective Jim Westlake

UNITED STATES DEPARTMENT OF JUSTICE
DRUG ENFORCEMENT ADMINISTRATION

RENO METROPOLITAN NARCOTIC TASK FORCE
4600 KIETZKE LANE
BUILDING I, SUITE 209
RENO, NEVADA 89502

June 25, 1980

Chief James Parker
Reno Police Department
P.O. Box 1900
Reno, Nevada 89502

Dear Chief Parker:

On June 23, 1980, the Reno Office of the Drug Enforcement Administration terminated a lengthy investigation resulting in the arrest of
nine defendants in the Lake Tahoe/Reno, Las Vegas and New York areas.

That investigation which centered on the cocaine distribution activities
of Michael JONES, et al, resulted in federal grand jury indictments
which charged the defendants with the distribution of cocaine as well
as a variety of other related charges.

During the course of the investigation, Dr. Bradley Kuhns was called
upon by this office to assist in the interview of an essential witness
through the use of hypnosis. On three occasions, Dr. Kuhns responded
to this office and for rather lengthy periods, applied hypnotic
techniques to the witness which resulted in the gathering of information
which would have other wise been most difficult, if not impossible, to
obtain.

I would like to take this opportunity to commend, through you, the
efforts of Dr. Kuhns in that regard. Not only was he able to develop
the information that we required, but at the same time demonstrated
his professional capabilities and expertise in that particular field.

Please convey my best regards to Dr. Kuhns and wishes for continued
success in the future.

Very truly yours,

Stephen M. Swanson
Resident Agent in Charge

cc: Dr. B. Kuhns

199

Met murder suspect arrested

NEW YORK (AP) — Police say gumshoe footwork, including the questioning of 1,000 people, led to the arrest Saturday of a 21-year-old stagehand on a charge of murder in the death of a violinist found nude, bound and gagged at the Metropolitan Opera House.

Craig Steven Crimmins, a Bronx high school dropout who worked backstage at the Lincoln Center opera house for four years, was arraigned Saturday afternoon in Manhattan Criminal Court and entered no plea. He was ordered held without bond.

He was charged in the death of Helen Hagnes Mintiks, who died when she was flung down an airshaft from the roof of the opera house.

Crimmins' father, Edward, has been an electrician at the prestigious opera house for 20 years. On the night of the slaying, police said, the younger Crimmins was working as a "grip," a handler of stage materials.

Edward Crimmins said his son was "a very friendly kid" who "couldn't hurt a fly." He charged his son had been "railroaded" by police.

Detectives in charge of the case said they had no motive for the killing and it was not clear whether young Crimmins and the victim knew each other. They said they believe a chance encounter backstage at the opera house preceded the killing.

The freelance violinist left the orchestra pit after the first act of a performance by the Berlin Ballet on July 23, apparently hoping to meet the ballet's star during intermission.

She never returned, and her body was found the next day. Police believe she was sexually attacked, and the medical examiner said she died from the fall.

Chief of Detectives James Sullivan would not say how police came to arrest Crimmins. He said the inquiry, which involved 16 detectives full time and as many as 50 detectives at various times, was not over.

Sullivan would neither confirm nor deny published reports that suspicion had turned to the stagehand because none of the other 250 Met employees or performers could substantiate Crimmins' account of his whereabouts the night of July 23.

Police would not make public a sketch used in questioning 1,000 performers and Met employees, both here and in Washington, D.C., where the Berlin dancers next appeared.

The sketch was drawn from the description given by a hypnotized witness, who spotted Mrs. Mintiks on a backstage elevator with an unidentified man the night she died

The chief said Crimmins looked like the sketch and that detectives had their eye on the stagehand for

Sketch of Craig Crimmins who was arrested Saturday and charged with the murder of a violinist at the Metropolitan Opera House.

"a couple of weeks".

"We don't know exactly how the two individuals may have been related at this time," Sullivan said.

"At this point, we don't think the crime was committed with a weapon," although a weapon may have been used at some point in the encounter, he said.

Detective Michael Struk of the 20th Precinct, who made the arrest, said Crimmins offered no resistance and was "unemotional" when officers took him into custody at his Bronx home.

Struk described Crimmins as 5-foot-8, 160 pounds, brown hair, blue eyes and "not particularly" muscular. He worked at the Met for three weeks after the slaying then began a month's vacation.

Crimmins lives with his father and 19-year-old sister in the Bedford Park section of the Bronx.

Los Angeles Times   Dec. 27, 1979

STRANGLER MURDERS

6 Minutes Into Hypnosis, Bianchi Implicates Buono

By BILL FARR
Times Staff Writer

It took Kenneth Bianchi only 6 minutes and 24 seconds under hypnosis to begin implicating his cousin, Angelo Buono Jr., as his partner in the Hillside Strangler murders.

Actually, it was Bianchi's supposed alter ego, "Steve Walker," who began talking about Buono's alleged role in the 10 killings.

"We took turns with all of them," Bianchi told the first of his six court-appointed psychiatric examiners in March.

Providing further details about the grisly 1977-78 slayings to another examiner a month later, Bianchi as "Steve" boasted, "What a team we were."

That psychiatrist, Dr. Ralph Allison of Davis, Calif., asked why Buono took part in the killings. "Steve" replied:

"He was just an easy guy to get with the program, you know. I gave him the idea and he went with it all the way. He's my kind of person. We should have more people like that in this world and we'd have less problems."

Then Allison asked, "Well, how did you two decide to kill girls in the first place." Came the reply:

"Just sitting around shooting the —. I asked Angelo if he ever killed anybody . . . He said, 'I don't know, why do you want to know?' I said, 'Well, what does it feel like?' He said, 'I don't know?' I said, 'Well, we should find out sometime.' He said, 'Sure. OK.' And we did."

These statements came during 56 hours of videotaped psychiatric examinations over a six-month period in Bellingham, Wash.

Bianchi was arrested there Jan. 12 for the murders of two Western Washington University women students. He has since pleaded guilty to those killings and admitted his role in Los Angeles' Strangler slayings.

In return for not receiving the death penalty, Bianchi has agreed to turn state's evidence against Buono in the Los Angeles case. Buono, who was arrested and charged with 10 murders plus pimping, pandering and extortion, has pleaded not guilty to all charges.

Buono's attorneys immediately raised the question of Bianchi's credibility and James Brustman, who heads the defense team, told The Times that the videotaped psychiatric sessions in Billingham will play a crucial role in arguing the credibility issue.

Of the six experts who examined Bianchi in Washington, two became convinced he had a genuine multiple personality, two decided he was faking, and two were undecided.

At the outset of the Washington examinations of Bianchi, he claimed total ignorance of the Bellingham and Los Angeles string of strangulations.

But in hypnosis sessions with three different examiners, "Steve" emerged and declared five of the Strangler murders were committed by Buono and the remainder by himself. "Steve" said both took part in all 10 but alternated at pulling cords around the victims' necks.

In these sessions, while "Steve" brashly told of the killings, Ken seemed mystified when asked about them and claimed ignorance of all the slayings.

Under examination by Dr. Martin Orne, director of the Pennsylvania Hospital's Institute of Experimental Psychiatry, a third personality named "Billy" emerged.

At first "Billy" knew only "Steve" and said he was not aware of Ken. But later he said he had gotten in touch with Ken.

In these hypnosis sessions, "Billy" talked about prostitution activities of Bianchi and Buono but attributed Bianchi's participation to "Steve."

In an apparent trance, "Billy" had this exchange with Orne.

Orne: What did Angelo do?

Billy: Angelo set up a lot of appointments for the girls.

Orne: Did he use them himself?

Billy: I don't know. I don't know. I don't think so.

Orne: Steve told me Angelo had a thing about not using girls himself that he ran as prostitutes.

Billy: I just don't know.

Orne: Did you get along with Angelo?

Billy: I didn't bother with him. It's really strange, because it's so hard to say there's anybody that could be like Steve. But Angelo comes about as close as you can get.

Throughout the videotaped hypnotic sessions, "Steve" was mean in his manner, profane in his language and appeared to be in utter contempt of any moral standards.

By contrast, Ken was unfailingly polite, soft-spoken and expressed respect for the laws of society.

Sometime near the end of April, Bianchi said that recollections of his involvement came flooding back to him while he was in his cell—not under hypnosis and without any help from a psychiatrist.

It was such a shock for him, he claimed, that he decided to commit suicide. However, he said he changed his mind after actually starting his own hanging.

By May 2, in a session with Bellingham psychiatrist Dr. Charles W. Moffet, Bianchi was able to relate considerable detail about the murders. At no time did Moffet put Bianchi under hypnosis.

Telling of his newly gained recollection of the murders, Bianchi had this conversation with Moffet:

Bianchi: With California for some reason, the faces are not as clear as here in Bellingham.

Moffet: The faces of the girls?

Bianchi: Right, and even the face of my cousin . . . but the faces are not 100% clear.

Moffet: He participated, your cousin, in these killings?

Bianchi: Very actively, yes.

Then Bianchi told the psychiatrist about the first killing and said the victim was a black girl—seemingly an account of the Oct. 17, 1977, murder of Yolanda Washington.

Bianchi said that Buono dropped him off on a street corner and said he was going to pick up a "hooker." When Buono returned, he already had had intercourse with the woman and had her sitting in the front seat of his car, according to Bianchi.

Continuing with his account, Bianchi said, "Buono flashed a badge on her and told her he was a cop . . . we made her get into the back seat . . . she was yelling and screaming.

Bianchi went on to say that the girl was handcuffed by Buono and that he (Bianchi) raped her as they drove along a freeway.

"I can practically hear him yelling, 'Get rid of her, get rid of her, kill her,'" Bianchi added.

"She was put on the floor and killed. No questions asked. No reason why."

Bianchi said he was not too clear on how she was strangled but he thought it was with her own blouse.

The victim was stripped of all her jewelry and clothing, Bianchi said. The jewelry was thrown into some bushes and the clothing, as with virtually all the victims, was discarded deep into a trash bin at Buono's auto upholstery shop in Glendale, Bianchi said.

Bianchi said the entire incident took about three hours, including dropping the victim's body off Barham Road in Los Angeles.

Moffet moved the discussion to the subsequent series of nine Los Angeles killings but did not seek details of each murder.

Moffet: Were they always with Angelo's participation?

Bianchi: Always. Every single one

Moffet: Always with the same technique? Strangulation?

Bianchi: Uh . . . yes.

In discussing why Buono would participate in the killings, Bianchi gave this appraisal of his cousin to Moffet:

"He has no respect for life. For other people. All he thinks of . . . . all he cares about is himself. He has screwed over a lot of people. He has

even pimped girlfriends of his. Girls he's going out with . . ."

On May 28, during an examination session with Orne, Bianchi gave this account of the killing of Cindy Hudspeth, the last of the Strangler victims, slain in February, 1978.

Bianchi said she went to Buono's shop for seat covers or floor mats for her car.

Bianchi began his account of the murder by saying:

"Angelo was in the house talking to the girl ... I came in and grabbed her around the throat . . . nothing's said . . . Angelo got up and went to get some rope, tied her and gagged her . . ."

Then there was a long sigh and Bianchi asked for a rest, saying: "This is very hard for me . . ."

Miss Hudspeth was blindfolded and ordered to remove her clothes. After both men raped her, Bianchi said, she was tied hand and foot.

"A rope was put around her neck and she was strangled," he recalled.

At this point, Bianchi can be heard on the tape whispering to himself, "What a cruel thing to do."

Miss Hudspeth's nude body was stuffed into the trunk of her car, which Bianchi said he drove. Bianchi said Buono followed in a second auto, to a spot on the Angeles Crest Highway above La Crescenta. There they pushed the car down a cliff, he said.

Bianchi is now in Los Angeles County Jail and is again having to relive the murders. This time it is during detailed interrogation sessions with police and prosecutors preparing for the upcoming trial of Buono.

To prepare for those proceedings, Bianchi also has literally been retracing the murderous steps he says he and his cousin took. This has been done during secret nighttime treks with detectives at his side.

FBI Instructs Agents In Hypnosis

CHICAGO (AP) – The FBI has drawn up guidelines and instructed agents in the use of hypnosis during questioning of witnesses or crime victims, agents say.

"The bureau wants the public to know exactly what we are doing, before someone discovers it accidently, misinterprets it, and blows it competely out of proportion." Robert Scigalski, a Chicago FBI agent, said in a story published in today's editions of the Chicago Tribune.

The FBI conducted a four-day seminar on the theory, history and uses of hypnosis in interviewing witnesses earlier this month in Quantico, Va.

Scigalski said the FBI guidelines for use of hypnosis are similar to those used by the Los Angeles police department, which has utilized the tactic for a number of years.

"It must be made clear from the start that a person cannot be hypnotized if he or she does not consent," said Scigalski.

A SEMANTIC "SHOPPING LIST"
FOR HYPNOTISTS

CAREFREE	GIVE WAY
SIGH OF RELIEF	PACIFIED
UNTROUBLED	THAW
MELLOW	COZY
ENJOYABLE FEELING	PASSIVE
LOOSE	TIRED
LIMP	HEAVY-EYED
LIMBER	DOZING
FLACCID	SLUMBER
LISTLESS	DROP OFF
LANGUID	DROWSY
SETTLE DOWN	REST
DREAMY	PAUSE
CONTENT	DRIFT
QUIET	RESTFUL
PLEASURABLE	SOOTHED
GOOD FEELING	BEAUTIFUL FEELING

Subconscious observers

Hypnosis lets witnesses remember crime details

LONDON (UPI) — When Israeli police found the bomb in the bus, the driver said he had no idea how it could have been placed aboard his vehicle. The Criminal Identification Division of the Israeli police then called in a psychotherapist.

Under hypnosis, Israeli police experts related in an article in the Journal of Forensic Science, the driver was able to reconstruct the entire route "and report every small event and detail which took place.

"He reported that upon arriving at a certain bus stop a dark-skinned youth entered the bus carrying a parcel. When the driver handed him his change he noticed a cold sweat on the young man's palm. Therefore, during hypnosis, he pointed out the youth as being a likely suspect.

"Although the driver only faced the youth for the short period of time needed to sell him a ticket, he was able to reconstruct an Identikit portrait. At a later date a suspect, whose description perfectly fitted the Identikit portrait, was arrested and confessed to the crime," the article said.

The Israelis marked their article "preliminary communication" —meaning it is subject to still more experimentation. They also cautioned that the technique should only be used on witnesses or victims who wish to cooperate fully and never on suspects except at their specific request and in the presence of an attorney.

From the 40 cases thus far studied, the authors said, it appears that hypnosis may be a potential tool to elicit essential information providing it is used by experts and the questioning relates to meaningful material.

The subconscious evidently cannot be bothered to dredge up inconsequentials.

The two techniques used to achieve "hyperamnesia" — memory recall greater than that achieved in a non-hypnotic state — are "age regression" and "revivification." In age regression, a subject is taken back in time to recall events of his past life. In revivification the subject relives or reexperiences earlier events.

The Scientific Interrogation Unit of the Israeli Police began using hypnotic techniques in 1973, the article said, and since then has recovered such relevant information from eyewitnesses and complainants as description of suspects, vehicles, license numbers, weapons and so on

A significant improvement in memory recall was credited to hypnosis in 24 of the first 40 cases in which the technique was used.

Los Angeles, Times   June 16, 1979

Teacher Describes Rape Suspect Under Hypnosis

The elementary school teacher who was beaten and sexually assaulted in her empty classroom June 5 underwent hypnosis in order to describe her attacker for a new composite drawing that was released by police Friday.

Judy Hodgins said she was willing to tell her story and submit to hypnosis because she is "representing other teachers of our school in seeking better protection."

The 34-year-old second-grade teacher had summoned help during the attack by ringing a campus alarm that no one at the 135th Street Elementary School answered.

This latest composite drawing has led investigators to suspect the man may be involved in the recent rape-robberies of two other Los Angeles teachers.

"But right now we don't have enough information to definitely say it is the same man," Det. Morton Duff said Friday.

Ms. Hodgins described her attacker as a black male between the ages of 18 and 20. The new composite drawing resembles the description of a man who raped another teacher at Budlong Elementary on May 26 and who shot and sexually assaulted Los Angeles High School teacher Miriam Schneider, 33, two days later, investigators said.

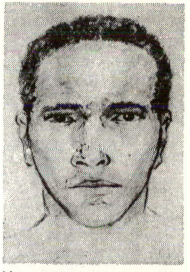

New composite drawing of the man who assaulted a teacher.

All three teachers had been working alone in their classrooms when they were attacked.

Ms. Hodgins' hypnois session uncovered additional details of the attack that Duff declined to disclose because they are "key points."

Persons with information concerning the teacher rape-robberies are urged to notify investigators at 485-6911.

207

Hypnosis helps boy recall face of his mother's killer

By Mitch Margo
Herald Examiner staff writer

The 9-year-old Costa Mesa boy who saw his mother's killer during one of the baffling Orange County "basher" attacks was hypnotized to help him recall the man's face, Police Lt. Jack Calnon said yesterday.

According to what Joey Carleton told police, the man walked straight toward him and was not wearing a mask.

"He just walked out the door and very gently moved the boy aside," Calnon said.

Something woke Joey last Sept. 14, the night his mother Marolyn was murdered.

"He woke up in the middle of the night and got a look at a man standing in his doorway," Calnon said. "Later he saw the man coming out of his mother's room."

Calnon said the boy got a clear look at the man's face and can recognize him, as can another witness whose description helped police make a composite drawing of the killer.

Joey's description was "fairly close" to that given by the other witness, and he has seen the composite drawing and "he says it kind of looks like him," Calnon said.

The child is under protective surveillance of police investigating six Orange County bludgeon murders, said Calnon.

Joey's mother, a 31-year-old widow, was not raped, as were some of the other victims, Calnon said. The five other victims included two in Costa Mesa, one in Irvine, one in Newport Beach and one in Tustin.

Police say the six women died of crushed skulls in a series of attacks beginning Aug. 2, 1977. The latest murder occurred Oct. 21. Two murders were on the same street in Costa Mesa.

"We feel all the attacks were perpetrated by the same man," Calnon said. Investigators have been sifting through more than 700 clues, he said.

"Of that, we have six or seven men we are looking at (as suspects). We are backgounding these people," he said. "We don't have enough to bring them in for a lineup."

Calnon said the suspects don't know they are being watched.

The Los Angeles Hillside Strangler Task Force has helped Orange County detectives organize their search for the mass-murderer, Calnon said.

GLOSSARY OF TERMS

ABREACTION — The release of emotionally charged material from the mental process.

AFFECT — Feeling tone; the feeling of emotion.

AGE PROGRESSION — Advancing the subject's age in the hypnotic trance.

AGE REGRESSION — The lowering of the subject's age level while in the hypnotic trance.

AMNESIA — The loss of memory. The amnesia which frequently occurs in hypnosis may be either spontaneous or induced by suggestion.

ANAESTHESIA — Insensibility to feelings or pain.

ANALYZE — To study the factors of a situation in detail in order to determine a solution or outcome.

ANIMAL MAGNETISM — Mesmerism; the principles advocated by Frederich Anton Mesmer.

ANIMATION, SUSPENDED — Temporary suspension of the vital functions.

ANIMOSITY — Resentment tending toward hostile action.

ANXIETY — Painful uneasiness of mind.

AUTOCONDITIONING — A series of experiments designed for bringing one's subconscious under control.

AUTOHYPNOSIS — Self-hypnosis; automatic hypnosis.

AUTOMATIC CONTROL — The controlling of one's mental processes automatically.

AUTOMATIC NERVOUS SYSTEM — A part of the peripheral nervous system regulating involuntary responses especially those concerned with nutritive, vascular and reproductive activities.

AUTOSUGGESTION — Self-suggestion, as distinguished from suggestions coming from another.

BAQUET — French word for tub; a device used by Mesmer for use in the induction of convulsions.

BLIND SPOT — An area in one's discernment where one fails to exercise understanding.

BRAIDISM — Those theories advocated by James Braid (Brade).

BRITISH ASSOCIATION — British medical group.

CATALEPTIC — A muscular seizure.

CATALEPTIC RIGIDITY — Muscle rigidity; number ten (10) on the Davis-Husband scale.

CATALEPTIC TRANCE — The second stage of hypnotic sleep; medium trance state.

CAUSATIVE FACTORS — The conditions leading to the development of mental and physical disorders.

CLAIRVOYANCE — The ability claimed by some individuals to discern objects not actually present.

CONDITIONED REFLEX — A reflex that responds automatically.

CONDITIONED SUBJECT — A person who has been initiated to hypnotic induction.

CONDITIONING — A series of trance inductions making certain ideas or things acceptable to the subject's subconscious mind.

CONSCIOUS — State of being aware of an inward state or outside fact.

CONSCIOUS AUTOSUGGESTION — The persistence in consciousness of impressions gained through subconscious training.

CONSCIOUS DISTORTION — Responses to the senses lessened in degree by interference during consciousness.

CONSCIOUS LEVEL CONTROL — The principles of autosuggestion in the waking state.

CONSCIOUS RECALL — Memory.

CONVULSION — An involuntary general paroxysm of muscular concentration.

COUÉISM — The principles of autosuggestion as advocated by Emile Coué.

COUNTER REGRESSION — The process of returning from a regressed state to a normal state; this is a normal part of the process of waking from hypnosis.

210

COUNTER SUGGESTION — A suggestion which is made to counter the effect of suggestions which have been given to induce hypnosis.

DAVIS-HUSBAND SCALE — Chart for determining hypnotic trance depths.

DEFENSE MECHANISM — A mode of behavior, or a belief, adopted by the subject, often unconsciously, to conceal the true state of matters pertaining to himself.

DISSOCIATION — The segregation from consciousness of certain components of mental processes, which then function independently.

DRUG HYPNOSIS (NARCOHYPNOSIS) — Sleep induced by narcotics (sodium amytal and sodium pentothal) aided by hypnotic suggestions.

DIANETICS — Science founded by mathematician Hubbard, utilizing, but not admitting to, some of the principles of hypnotism.
utilizing, but not admitting to, all the principles of hypnotism.

EFFECT — Created condition with hypnotic suggestions.

ELECTROENCEPHALOGRAPH — An apparatus for detecting and recording brain waves.

EMOTIONAL OUTLET — A habit pattern formed to release emotional tension.

EXCITORY PERSONALITY — One who stimulates or irritates an organ or tissue.

E.S.P. (EXTRA SENSORY PERCEPTION) — Perception which is not mediated by the sense organs.

EXTROVERT — One who interests himself with the outside world rather than himself.

FAITH HEALER — One who practices treatment of diseases by religious belief and prayer.

FASCINATION POINT — The object upon which the subject fixes his gaze in hypnotic method.

FATHER HYPNOSIS — The use of a forceful tone for inducing hypnotic sleep.

FLACCIDITY — A looseness; an absence of tone seen in muscles of persons relaxed in hypnosis.

FLUIDISM — Mesmer's theory of a life-sustaining fluid contained within each body.

FRACTIONATION — The procedure of hypnotizing the subject, waking him and rehypnotizing a number of times in the same session; an effective means of increasing trance depth.

FREE ASSOCIATION — Spontaneous unrestricted associations of loosely linked ideas or mental images having very little rational sequence or continuity.

GLOVE ANESTHESIA — A loss of sensation in an area corresponding to that covered by a glove.

HALLUCINATIONS — Perceptions arising in the absence of appropriate external stimuli.

HEMOPHILIAC — One who is affected by hereditary disease occurring only in males but transmitted genetically by females, characterized by excessive bleeding.

HETEROSUGGESTION — Sleep suggestions made by operator and directed to subject.

HYPNOANALYSIS — Hypnosis utilizing psychoanalytic techniques.

HYPNODISC — A disc with spirals used in inducing hypnotic sleep.

HYPNODONTICS — The science of dental hypnosis.

HYPNOGRAPHY — A technique in hypnoanalysis in which the hypnotized subject is brought to express psychological conflicts in painting.

HYPNOID — A state resembling sleep.

HYPNOS — Greek work for sleep.

HYPNOSIS — A science performed by an artist; name given to the sleep-state by Dr. James Braid; a repressed state of mental functioning in which ideas are accepted by suggestion rather than by logical evaluation.

HYPNOTHERAPY — Treatment by hypnosis.

HYPNOTIC INSURANCE — A predetermined code by the

operator transposed to his subject to return the subject to the hypnotic state instantly.

HYPNOTIC PASSES — Those gestures or movements made by the hypnotist over the body of the subject without actually touching him/her.

HYPNOTISM — The science of hypnosis.

HYPNOTIST — The operator.

HYPNOTIZE — The act of inducing hypnotic sleep.

HYSTERIA — Emotional excitability due to mental causes.

HYPERAESTHESIA — A high degree of sensitivity.

IDEOMOTOR ACTIVITY — Nonvoluntary movement produced as the direct expression of an idea.

INSTANT SLEEP SUGGESTION — A method of inducing sleep automatically in post-hypnotic control.

INTROVERT — One whose interests are directed inwardly upon himself.

KINAESTHETIC DELUSIONS — Total anesthesia.

LAY HYPNOTIST — The term applied to persons outside the medical profession who utilize hypnotic techniques in the practice.

LETHARGIC SLEEP — Light trance state, characterized by little or no post-hypnotic control; first trance state.

LETHARGY — A condition of drowsiness or stupor.

MAGNETISM — The belief, founded by Mesmer, in which the magnetic power of one human being could control another person.

MAGNETIZER — One who uses the first principles advocated by Mesmer.

MANIA — Excessive enthusiasm; a craze.

MASS HYPNOSIS — Trance induction of a group of people simultaneously.

MECHANICAL DEVICE — An object, such as a hypnodisc, used to induce the hypnotic trance.

MEDIUM — A person supposed to be susceptible to supernormal agencies and able to impart knowledge derived from them or to perform actions impossible without their aid.

MESMERISM — Those hypnotic principles advocated by Mesmer.

MESMERIST — One who employs the principles of Mesmerism.

METRONOME — An instrument used for marking exact time.

MODERATE EFFECT GROUP — Simple experiment that can be performed after reaching the relaxation stage of hypnosis, such as temperature changes.

MONOIDEISM — A term employed by Braid for waking-hypnosis and the lighter stages of hypnotic sleep.

MOTHER HYPNOSIS — Soft, lulling tones used to induce hypnosis.

MOTIVATION — The force which determines pattern of behavior.

MOTOR ACTIVITY — Designating or pertaining to a nerve or nerve fiber which passes from the central nervous system or a ganglion to a muscle and by the impulse which it transmits or causes movement.

NERVOUS SLEEP — The hypnotic state wherein conscious is inactive while subconscious is alert and suggestible.

NORMAL SLEEP — The state wherein the conscious sleeps normally.

OBJECTIVITY — Ability to view events, ideas and phenomena as external and apart from self-consciousness, detached and impersonal.

OCCULT — The unseen; beyond the bounds of ordinary knowledge.

OPERATOR — Hypnotist.

PAIN — A distressing feeling.

PANACEA — A cure-all.

PHENOMENON — An exceptional, unusual, or abnormal thing or occurrence.

PHOBIA — A morbid, exaggerated, unreasonable fear.

PHRENOLOGY — The study of the conformation of the skull as indicative of mental faculties.

POSTHYPNOTIC SUGGESTION — Those suggestions made

during and after the hypnotic trance to be carried out
after awakening.

POST-TRANCE CONDITION — Enrapport state in which the
subject maintains a certain degree of susceptibility consciously.

PRECONDITIONING — The psychological impression you
make on your subject concerning hypnosis.

PREHYPNOTIC SUGGESTION — A visual or verbal suggestion used to indicate trance conditions.

PREHYPNOTIC TESTS — Tests based on reflexes accompanied by suggestion to create certain effects.

PROFESSIONAL HYPNOTIST — One who makes a living
employing the principles of hypnotism.

PROJECTION — The attributing of one's own feeling to
someone else.

PSYCHOANALYSIS — A method of evaluating persistent
subconscious ideas.

PSYCHOLOGICAL CRUTCH — Leaning heavily on another
person to create certain effects.

PSYCHOSIS — Any serious mental derangement.

PSYCHOSOMATIC — Functional inter-relationship between
mind and body.

RAPPORT — Relation of harmony, comfort, accord; state of
being in tune with your subject.

RATIONALIZATION — To evaluate with adequate analysis.

REFLEXIVE TESTS — See Prehypnotic Tests.

REINCARNATION — The belief in successive returns to
physical life.

RIGIDITY — Muscular tenseness.

SCHOOL OF NANCY — Those ideas sponsored by A. A.
Liebeault and H. Bernheim; the establishment of scientific
hypnosis so called for its geographic location in Nancy,
France.

SELF CONTROL — Conscious autosuggestion.

SELF HYPNOSIS — Placing one's self into a trance state.

SELF RAPPORT — Being in tune with one's self.

SHOCK TREATMENT — A doubtful method of therapy using electric current to induce an artificial state of shock.

SKEPTIC — One who doubts or disbelieves.

SLEEP INDUCTION — Inducing the hypnotic trance.

SLEEP RECORDINGS — Records and tapes prepared for use in inducing a hypnotic trance.

SODIUM PHENOBARBITAL — A drug used in narcohypnosis.

SOMNAMBULISTIC TRANCE — A state of deep sleep; third and final trance state; usually the hypnotist's objective with his subjects.

STAGE HYPNOTISM — Entertaining hypnotism.

SUBCONSCIOUS — The nature of mental operation not yet present in consciousness.

SUBCONSCIOUS CONTROL — Automatic suggestion.

SUBJECT — One who is experimented with or tested.

SUGGESTION — An idea which is offered to the subject for acceptance.

SUGGESTIVE THERAPY — The removal of symptoms by hypnotic suggestion.

SUSCEPTIBILITY — Capability of receiving impressions; sensability.

SUSPENDED ANIMATION — See Animation, Suspended.

SYMPTOM REMOVAL — Removal of pain that keynotes a condition.

THERAPEUTIC — Of or pertaining to the healing arts; curative.

TIME DISTORTION — Unexplainable lapse of time during the trance by the subject.

TRANCE — A state of profound abstraction.

TRANCE CONDITION — The state of being hypnotized.

TRANCE DEPTH — The level of sleep achieved by the subject.

TRANCE DURATION — Time spent in the hypnotic state.

TRANCE MEDIUM — The use of a hypnotized subject to forsee the future.

TRANSFERENCE — The self-made science of Professor J.M. Charcot.

TRAUMA — Injury; shock of the resulting condition.

TWILIGHT SLEEP — The state between consciousness and natural sleep.

VASOMOTOR — Physical activity over which the subject has no control.

WAKING HYPNOSIS — Hypnotic suggestions accepted by the subject in the waking state.

WORD ASSOCIATION — Mental and emotional reaction to word stimuli.

RECOMMENDED BOOKS

Barnett, Edgar, M.D., *Unlock Your Mind and Be Free With Hypnotherapy*......................$10.95

Block, Eugene, *Hypnosis: A New Tool in Crime Detection* 7.95

Cheek, David, M.D. & LeCron, L., *Clinical Hypnotherapy*, New York: Grune & Stratton, Inc., 1968 15.00

Clement, Pierre, *Hypnosis And Power Learning* 6.95

Cooke & Van Vogt, *Hypnotism Handbook*......... 12.50

Elman, Dave, *Hypnotherapy*.................... 17.50

Gibson, Prof., *Hypnosis: Its Nature And Therapeutic Uses*.................................. 10.00

Kappas, John, *The Professional Hypnotism Manual* .. 17.50

Kuhns, Bradley, "A View of Human Behavior," *Journal of California Association of Polygraph Examiners*, 1980.........................

Kuhns, Bradley, "Physiological Functions of the Brain" *Journal of California Association of Polygraph Examiners*, 1979.........................

McGill, Ormond, *Hypnotism and Mysticism of India* 11.50

McGill, Ormond, *Professional Stage Hypnotism* 15.00

Morris, Freda, Ph.D., *Hypnosis With Friends And Lovers*.................................. 5.95

Mutke, Peter, M.D., *Selective Awareness*........... 5.95

Tebbetts, Charles, *Self-Hypnosis And Other Mind Expanding Techniques* 3.95

Wolberg, L., *Hypnoanalysis,* New York: Grune & Stratton, Inc., 1945.........................

Wolberg, L., *Medical Hypnosis,* New York: Grune & Stratton, Inc., 1945. . . . .

Wolberg, L., *The Principles of Hypnotherapy,* Volumes I & II, New York: Grune & Stratton, Inc., 1948 . .

Wycott, James, *Franz Anton Mesmer/Between God And The Devil*. 5.95

Available through Westwood Publishing Co.

For Free Catalog, write to:

312 Riverdale Dr., Glendale, CA 91204
(213) 242-1159

You Can Activate the Power of Your Subconscious Mind and...
COME ALIVE!
with SELF HYPNOSIS and "POWER PROGRAMMING"
by Gil Boyne
Authority on Hypnosis Motivation and Mental Programming

CASSETTE TAPE #101 — SELF-CONFIDENCE THROUGH SELF-IMAGE PROGRAMMING
Radiate dynamic self-confidence — Improve your self-image — Overcome the fear of criticism, fear of rejection, fear of failure — Feel more lovable and appreciate yourself more   **$9.95**

CASSETTE TAPE #102 — CONCENTRATION — MEMORY — RETENTION — PERFECT RECALL
This method is the only scientifically-validated memory system known — requires no memorization of key words or word associations — liberate your photographic memory — a fool-proof cure for forgetfulness — use your automatic mind search and memory-scanning capacity. The unique methods are placed indelibly into your subconscious mind for your permanent use.   **$9.95**

CASSETTE TAPE #103 — DEEP RELAXATION AND RESTFUL SLUMBER
Here is a new way to go to sleep! This incredibly effective and totally safe technique enables you to shed the cares of the day and drift off within minutes after your head hits the pillow. Your float into a sleep as refreshing and rejuvenating as it is deep. You feel new vitality and energy each morning, and you maintain high energy levels through the day.   **$9.95**

CASSETTE TAPE #104 — SECRETS OF SUCCESS ATTITUDES
Overcomes your subconscious "will to fail" — you can learn to move rapidly toward your career and financial goals — success and riches spring from a foundation of "subconscious mental expectancy" — money does not come from high IQ, education, hard work or goodness — begin now to realize the enduring success and wealth that is potentially yours!   **$9.95**

CASSETTE TAPE #105 — TRIM AND FIT — VITAL AND HEALTHY
The mental factors in compulsive overeating are widely recognized. This new method conditions your nervous system and your subconscious mind to rapidly move you toward your goal of attractive fitness. Gives you a new self-image about your physical self. Changes your eating habits by changing your appetite desires. Improves your figure easily and quickly.   **$9.95**

CASSETTE TAPE #106 — SECRETS OF COMMUNICATION AND EXPRESSION
How to present your ideas in a way that insures acceptance. If you are the one who feels fear and tension at the thought of having to give a speech or a short report, this tape is a blessing! You can speak with absolute confidence and perfect poise, whether to an audience of hundreds or a small group or a single person.   **$9.95**

CASSETTE TAPE #107 — DYNAMICS OF CREATIVE ACTING
Program your mind for success in your acting career. Covers auditions, rehearsing, performing, mental attitude and self-image. Overcome, "The Freeze," learn lines quickly and easily. Express your creativity.   **$9.95**

CASSETTE TAPE #108 — DYNAMICS OF SELF-DISCOVERY
Answers the question, "WHO AM I?"! Overcomes the identity crisis. Creates a powerful belief in your own abilities. Discover the real self and your true capacity for joyful living! Teaches you how to give yourself — love, acceptance and approval.   **$9.95**

CASSETTE TAPE #109 — DYNAMIC HEALTH AND RADIANT VITALITY
You can overcome fears and negative beliefs and your state of health. This program subconsciously develops the mental imagery, feeling tone, and mental expectancy for radiant, vibrant expression of perfect health.

CASSETTE TAPE #112 — DYNAMICS OF CREATIVE WRITING
The hypnotic programming tape that was developed for a producer-writer of a famous dramatic-comedy T.V. show. This writer later claimed that this programming was an important factor in the creation of a script that won an Emmy nomination.   **$9.95**

 CASSETTE TAPE #114 — YOU CAN STOP SMOKING NOW!
This power-programmed cassette will overcome the helpless feeling that underlies tobacco addiction. In just a short time, you become free of tobacco -- permanently! Enjoy a longer, healthier, happier life.   **$9.95**

 CASSETTE TAPE #115 — SEXUAL ENRICHMENT FOR MEN
You have the right to sexual happiness! Powerful desire, total function, and glowing fulfillment is the result of your use of this program.   **$9.95**

CASSETTE TAPE #116 — SEXUAL ENRICHMENT FOR WOMEN
See description above for #115.   **$9.95**